NAVIGATING
THE DARK SIDE
OF WEALTH

NAVIGATING
THE DARK SIDE
OF WEALTH
A Life Guide for Inheritors

THAYER CHEATHAM WILLIS

NEW CONCORD PRESS
PORTLAND, OREGON

New Concord Press
P. O. Box 3825
Portland, Oregon 97208-3825

Copyright © 2003, 2005 by Thayer Cheatham Willis

Second impression. With a new introduction.

The author gratefully acknowledges Easton Press for permission to
reprint their translation of Aesop's "The Dog and the Wolf."

Editor: Lionel Fisher
Proofreader: Marvin Moore
Design: Martha Gannett
Composition: William H. Brunson Typography Services
Printing: Dynagraphics

Printed in the United States of America

Library of Congress Control Number 2002094980
ISBN 0-9725494-0-4

For Jon, Julianne, and Clay

Contents

Foreword

CONTRARY TO GENERAL CULTURAL and popular belief that wealth
and money can cure most of the ills of individuals, families, and
communities, Thayer Cheatham Willis, a trained psychotherapist,
has set forth a very challenging thesis that this premise is not true.
The author, herself born to wealth and an inheritor of wealth,
has written *Navigating the Dark Side of Wealth: A Life Guide for
Inheritors*. Using the case studies of many of her clients (with
fictionalized names), who have faced problems of family relation
ships, job relationships, etc., she testifies that there are many
reasons why inheritors of wealth have not always turned out to be
happy people.

The author knew generally that upon the passing of her
father, Julian Cheatham, she and her family would inherit considerable financial support, but she never understood or had any
specific information to permit her to plan accordingly. She points
out that oftentimes this has been illustrated in the course of her
professional work with clients, when fathers and husbands have
failed to fully share the financial status of the family. In some
circumstances, it means that money could always be available, but
without the recipient knowing the parameters or scale of spending priorities or limits.

Thayer Willis has stated very specifically that she herself made
many destructive choices that were of her own free will, but she

was able to make restorative decisions and undertake the arduous journey back when she embraced her spirituality.

She convincingly communicates that the fundamental value(s) of life you treasure most can ultimately become your god. She quotes the biblical injunction of Matthew 19:24–26, which says, "It is easier for a camel to go through the eye of a needle than for a rich person to enter the kingdom of God." But "with God all things are possible."

To me, as a first-time reader of her manuscript, I quickly sensed that the author has superb professional training as a psychotherapist. At the same time, she possesses great sensitivity to matters of the spirit and to the spiritual truths that round out the total person's education—mind, body, and spirit. Today we live in a very secularized society with great emphasis on materialism. One could say that accumulation of worldly goods dominates many of our public and private goals. It is refreshing to note that in this book, one can easily discern a balance between the material and the spiritual. This is not a matter of either/or, but simply the blending of the author's experience, wisdom, and sensitivity.

For example, in the ways of bringing up children, she suggests teaching them the importance of sharing and giving and to judge life not by what they can get as much as what they are in a position to give. Therefore, parents will find examples in this tome, or perhaps even solace, that a more normal life is possible, despite the threat of overabundance.

I think those of us who are not inheritors of wealth will appreciate more clearly the values of family, friendship, and community that ultimately can be measured in terms of great blessing, which is another kind of wealth.

People who are inheritors of wealth will find guidance that will surely point to a more fulfilling life, knowing who their friends are and enjoying life without suspicion or testing, because of greater security.

In the Gospel of Matthew relating to the eye of a needle, Jesus did *not* say rich people could not get into heaven. Rather, he taught that oftentimes they don't recognize and cannot see or hear the call to love God, and their neighbor as themselves, when blinded by worldly possessions and wealth.

Thayer Willis gives us opportunity to pause and to reflect on the problems we all face at some times in our lives—and recognition of the good things of life we often miss, either because of greed or our focus only on the temporal things. She has experienced discoveries and imparts them with grace, insight, and charm.

Mark O. Hatfield
PORTLAND, OREGON

Acknowledgments

I HAVE GATHERED THE STORIES and experiences for this book throughout my life and especially over the past fourteen years. There are many clients, acquaintances, and friends without whom the book could not be the collection of lessons that it is. It was so hard to bring it all together with focus that at times I thought it was not meant to be. But God continued to light my path in the direction of the book you now hold in your hands, and my greatest hope is that in it you will find the counsel, information, and inspiration to make your life better.

My father, Julian N. Cheatham, now deceased, and my mother, Alyce R. Cheatham, gave me excellent guidance in my values, priorities, and education. They held up high standards for me, and because they did, the lasting benefits have shaped my life. They taught me by example to contribute to society, and my desire to do so has provided both the seed and the commitment to write this book. Their greatest gift to me was the teaching I received to develop my relationship with God.

All the stories in this book are based on truth, but for the sake of confidentiality, names and details have been changed. Any resemblance to real people or stories is coincidental.

The list of those to whom I am deeply grateful for their help is long: Jeff Auxier, Jan Bisenius, Barbara Blouin, Dave Bone, Kathy Calcagno, John Comerford, Kitty Dietrich, Barry Fisher,

Lionel Fisher, Martha Gannett, Marcia Garland, Walter Kingsbery, Celia Lubisich, Marvin Moore, Lark Palma, Bob Pamplin Jr., Katie Radditz, Mary Rowland, Myra Salzer, Bob Sanders, Howard Shapiro, Shauna Tweedy, and Bob Veres.

From the bottom of my heart I wish to thank my life partner and best friend, my husband, Jon. It was his seemingly endless patience during the creation of this book and his willingness at times to take over parenting responsibilities, which would ordinarily have been mine, that made it all possible.

Introduction

WHAT IS THE GOAL OF A LIFE? I once thought it defined by freedom, the freedom of the character Jason Robards plays in the movie called *A Thousand Clowns*. The clowns tramp the streets of Manhattan on their way to work each morning at an insurance brokerage, ad agency, department store, and bakery, while Robards's character, Murray, watches them, drinks another cup of coffee, and perhaps heads up to Central Park to buy a balloon.

Moviegoers in the late 1960s cherished this movie and its portrayal of a life with freedom to sing or paint or write or run through the park. But what happened to these free spirits? Most weighed the value of freedom versus the value of money. And money won. They trained as corporate lawyers and investment bankers and professors and doctors. Bought expensive houses and jewelry and vacations. Realized that they'd made a Faustian bargain. I recently met a guy at my husband's class reunion who told me he was "a poet stuck in a lawyer's body." Financial advisors tell me that most of their clients have plenty of money. What they can't find is the magic potion that brings satisfaction or fullness to a life.

I've spent a good deal of time thinking and writing about money and freedom over the past thirty years. That's how I came to "meet" Thayer Willis on the phone in January 1995 when I was writing a weekly column for the *Sunday New York Times*. Willis, an heir to the Georgia-Pacific lumber company fortune, has plenty of money. It took years for her to find freedom. The two are not mutually exclusive, but one doesn't guarantee the other, either. Luckily, Willis was willing—even eager—to talk about her journey, her personal demons, how circumstances led her through a string of psychiatric disorders and depression and what she might call brattiness and self-indulgence before she found the path to becoming a whole person. When she did, she went back to graduate school and became a therapist to counsel other wealthy people on their own search.

By the time I met Willis, I'd come to realize that most money decisions are based on emotions rather than dollars and sense, that the unhappiness surrounding money comes not from how much is available but how it is used. Most Americans fail to achieve what they could in life, fall short of realizing their dreams, not because of lack of money but because they don't understand what they want that money to buy.

Willis helped me to understand that money cannot buy this mystical freedom elixir. An heiress who grew up in one of the most beautiful neighborhoods in Portland, Oregon, Willis had no worries about saving for retirement or patching together the money to send her two children to college. What *did* she have to worry about? Guilt. Maybe she wasn't using her wealth in the best possible way. Suspicion. Perhaps people who befriended her were really after her money. Lack of self-worth. She hadn't done anything to earn the money. She wasn't forced to grapple with the trade-offs that teach expensive lessons. Willis needn't choose: Should I go to graduate school or save money to buy a house? Must I continue at this job when I detest my boss and feel compromised by him each day? Is it irresponsible to have a second child when money is so tight? What must I give up to get my dream house or once-in-a-lifetime vacation? Answers to these questions shape our lives. Willis could do it all. She needn't answer the questions.

We each give a nod to the truism that "Money doesn't buy happiness," yet when my column about Willis appeared with the headline, "The Troubles With Money," I received angry letters from readers: "Oh, give me a break. Poor little rich girl. I wouldn't have any trouble if I were a millionaire." So it is that Willis suffers a double whammy. Not only do people envy her wealth. But she gets no credit for the years of hard work she's done to create a life and to make peace with her money.

Money attitudes like these run deep in America. A couple of years ago, my daughter's small-town crew team hired a coach who had rowed at Harvard University and happened, by the way, to be the grandson of Thomas Watson, the founder of IBM. We live in New York's Hudson Valley—IBM country—and the coach quite naturally wanted to keep his identity private. He worked for minimum wage with this novice team, getting up at 4:30 A.M. in March to bundle up and wade into the freezing Hudson River, and he encouraged the athletes at meets, even though they were nearly hopeless in their inexperience. Everybody liked him. Admired him. Until they discovered who he was. Then many crew parents reacted predictably. "Why couldn't he do more for the team?" one parent wanted to know. "I didn't see any IBM money rolling into our treasury," another parent said. And another: "I never would have known he was rich. He certainly always was eager for his pay-check." Yes. He must have been looking for a way to create value and maybe even build self-esteem. Looking for a way to be paid for something he could do well.

Earned money, neutral money, money as a fair medium of exchange for value, is critical to each of us if we are to build a sat-isfying life. The attitude of the crew parents to the coach—they saw his connection to IBM as the solution to a financially struggling team—robs the rich of the luxury of learning how to set values, how to find a passion, how to create a unique journey through life and discover the growth and satisfaction that come from completing a circle.

When I first interviewed Willis, I felt an immediate camaraderie. Despite the fact that I'd grown up on the other side of the tracks. Or maybe because of it. Getting to know Willis became a stepping stone in my own journey, helping me to understand how each of us must work to free himself from the idea that money gives us our identity. I'd grown up in northern Minnesota, moving from one construction site to another in a camping trailer, living in houses without electricity or plumbing, as my father traveled to look for work. When I became a journalist in New York, I didn't treasure my own financial background any more than Willis treasured hers. Not that I necessarily wanted more money. But I wanted the polish and sophistication that came from owning a trust fund and polo ponies, the instinct to see that Nantucket is classier than Martha's Vineyard, the ability to recognize genuine Shaker furniture or Queen Anne chairs. New Yorkers have the sneakiest ways of discovering your status—whether you're an Upper West Sider or a Greenwich Villager—by asking about favorite restaurants, Broadway shows, vacation spots, and other questions that expediently divide people into layers of status. Read Kafka? TriBeCa. Eat Jello? Upper East Side.

The fact that Willis struggled with wealth as a child and I struggled with poverty isn't as different as one might expect. Several of Willis's childhood friends died. Accidents. Suicide. In northern Minnesota, desperate people—poor people who have trouble with money—are more likely to shoot themselves or a family member. What's the difference? I was struck by how similar our journeys, particularly our spiritual journeys, had been.

Willis and I didn't meet until the winter of 2004 when she came to New York because her family was staging Mozart's Requiem Mass at Carnegie Hall in honor of her uncle, who would have been 100 in 2002. Willis and I met for lunch at a French Thai restaurant in midtown. Not extravagant, not dowdy. She was waiting in the booth when I arrived. I sat down and felt a terror that I hadn't faced in years. Willis was just the same as she'd been on the phone. Charming. Funny. Yet in a way she—and her wealth—represented all the people I'd felt inferior to over the years. Her elegant glove-leather handbag I imagined to be custom-made in just the color and style she requested. My own tatty backpack looked huge and ungainly. My regular business clothes, which I'd comfortably worn to give a speech to five hundred people, looked shabby and ill-chosen, my comfortable walking shoes clunky and cheap. I doubt that Willis noticed my discomfort. I hope not. I'm certain she didn't find my wardrobe unacceptable. My problem was entirely of my own making. Had I not known that Willis was wealthy, that her family could hold a requiem mass at Carnegie Hall, I would have felt fine. Which is so often the trouble with money. It turns us into someone else, someone we don't want to be, even someone we've worked hard not to be.

Of course many people do have very real problems with a lack of money. They struggle to buy bread and pay the rent and clothe their children. Which is another cause of anxiety to the wealthy. To all of us, really. I sometimes feel that I shouldn't have anything extra until everyone in the world has enough. But how can I solve this problem? It's too big. What if I had enough money to solve the problem of starvation in a small country? What should I do with it? Who do I help? Having great wealth does not provide an answer to these troubling questions. Studies show that suddenly wealthy people—like lottery winners—end up miserable because they don't know how to make decisions about the money, because they lack that magical potion each of us needs to create a self that is about value rather than about money.

This is a book about conquering the dark side of wealth. It's a book about how to handle the loneliness and guilt and isolation suffered by people who have so much money that they need never work. It's a story told by a woman of wealth who wouldn't settle for self-indulgence and superficial relationships, who married, had two children, and works each day to grow her relationships with family members, to create value for others in the world who feel paralyzed by money, by their wealth.

Willis sees her audience as inheritors, those who have inherited so much money that they don't need to work. I see it as larger. Financial planners tell me the biggest problem they see among baby boomers is that they've created some wealth in their lives but no meaning. Now they're searching about for something to grab onto. A psychologist friend tells me that the wealthy people she sees have everything but values. When she asked a college student what her parents value, the girl thought and thought and finally came up with a list of material goods. A car. A beach house. Jewelry. Many advice givers are beginning to address this value void in their practices. They ask clients questions about their dreams, their passion, relationships, career. If you won the lottery, how would you change your life? If you had twenty-four hours to live, what would you most regret not doing?

Great questions. Willis has found her answers. Here she helps others find their own.

Mary Rowland
NEW YORK CITY, NEW YORK

The Dark Side of Wealth

YOU'RE AT A PARTY. Someone asks you casually, "So, what do you do?"

Most people just answer the question. But you're different, both in your circumstances and in your reaction. You experience a sense of panic, "Oh, no, not again! I *hate* that question!" You try to think of how to make a hobby sound like a profession. Words such as *nothing, parasite, fraud,* and *lost soul* leap to mind, along with concerns over how to make yourself sound like a responsible adult.

"Oh, I do a lot of things...," you reply finally with a weak smile. You almost add resentfully, "Well, I have money. I don't *have* to do anything."

Instead, you deflect attention from yourself by asking quickly, "And what is it *you* do?" suddenly feeling foolish and very self-conscious, the mood of the moment ruined. You hear little of the reply as you ask yourself miserably, "Does it show how little I do that is of any real value?"

An extreme reaction to an innocent circumstance? You may well think so, for unless you're an inheritor you may find it hard to relate to this story. But if you have inherited substantial wealth, then you know that it is harder for you than for most people to achieve a sense of purpose and competence.

For you, there is good news. It *is* possible for the wealthy to have such a conversation with confidence and enthusiasm. It might take some work to reach this place of guilt-free acceptance of your material ease, but it can be done.

The first step is to ask yourself, "What do I *want* to do?" Not "What do I *have* to do to be at peace with my wealth since most other people have to work hard for everything they have?"

When you deliberately ask yourself, "What is it I *want*?" other questions must follow to illuminate the path: "What do I already do that I enjoy and that is fulfilling to me?" "What other things would I like to try?" "Is there any reason why I can't do them?"

They have experienced and successfully navigated through what I call the Dark Side of wealth.

If you have an interest that you are aware of, then the question becomes, "Do I know anyone who could be my mentor in this?"

Asking yourself these questions is part of a step-by-step process through which you can intentionally structure what you do with your time—and, by so doing, build your *sense of purpose* in the world.

It can be done. People just like you and me are doing it all the time. In the process, they are refusing to accept the personal limitations imposed on them when they received what the outside world regards as a windfall.

They have experienced and successfully navigated through what I call the Dark Side of wealth.

Rebecca is a beautiful thirty-year-old woman whose inherited fortune has kept her childlike in every way but physically. (Her name and story have been fictionalized, as have the names and stories of the rest of the people depicted in this book, in order to protect their privacy.) During our first session, my immediate reaction—which I later saw as a classic example of countertransference—was a strong desire to protect her. As she continued in therapy with me, I had to fight the urge to give her a crash course in the realities of life while sheltering her the whole time.

Aimless, easily led, and transparently shallow, Rebecca remained unmotivated in therapy, sometimes canceling appointments well ahead of their scheduled dates. And although her stated objective was to determine what to do with her life, her usual affect was unfeigned apathy.

Her father was a strong person, she reported, with whom she had a positive connection, but none of her relationships with other men had lasted very long or had been very deep. Her immediate goal, she said, was marriage and a family with a partner who would respect and care for her.

Treatment consisted primarily of engaging her intellect and emotions in order to heighten the awareness of her present lifestyle in all its dimensions, attitudes, and behaviors. The sessions ended after thirteen months when she traveled to California to pursue a graduate program of study and to explore a relationship that seemed promising to her at the time.

Professional observations: I've had several of these aimless clients, and I'm always surprised that they come in at all. They tend to be likeable but challenging to me as a therapist. Certainly it is easier to work with more motivated individuals, and I have to remind myself that those who feel apathetic and purposeless (one of the common traits of children of wealth) deserve as much of a chance to fulfill themselves as anyone else.

For them, I can give a hand, reaching in to help them out of something they don't even realize surrounds them: the spirit-sapping dark side of wealth.

Other inheritors feel a need to work, yet they haven't found a way to do it that seems right.

Michelle is a case in point. She became my client when she was thirty-five, an inheritor whose father had been hugely successful in business. She herself had already started three very labor-intensive businesses. She was busy working most of the time, even though her father would give her money from her trusts whenever she wanted it. She felt that she should be as successful in business as her father had been. Sometimes her friends asked her, "Why do you work so hard? You don't have to work at all." She didn't really have an answer, except to say that she wanted to. What she told me was that she felt pressured to work hard, and she recognized that the pressure came from within herself. She was hoping to ease up on it, but she didn't know how.

Professional observations: *Sometimes daughters as well as sons feel driven by their father's big shadow to work as hard as he did (or does), and this pressure may be coming entirely from within. Often, inheritors believe they must do everything better than anyone else. After all, they've been given a big leg-up in life with all their opportunities and wealth. Surely, they think, the cynics of the world would need greater proof from them than from everyone else that they are worthwhile people.*

Trying to provide that proof, and always failing to live up to your own impossible standards, is one of the darkest corners of the dark side of wealth.

My inspiration to write this book came from different challenges than the ones presented in these stories. For years, I had been drawn into conversations at parties, on airplanes, during my children's sporting events, virtually everywhere I met new people, with the conversational gambit, "So, what do you do?" And my reaction was always the same.

Immediately, I'd ascertain what time it was and determine how soon I could finish talking with this individual while remaining civil. If I had no time, I'd simply reply, "Mainly, I'm a mom. I have two young children." If I had a few moments to spare and felt there was a reason to impart the nature of my profession, I'd add, "I'm also a psychotherapist, and I help people with the challenges of wealth." Then I'd leave some space for the person to make a bit of sense out of my morsel of information.

I bring this up now because I believe many will misunderstand the premise of this book. I'm used to seeing people visibly confused as they ponder what challenges financial abundance could possibly impose: *"Poor little rich kids? Give me a break!"*

I'm also well aware that many in our society resent the rich. One of my objectives, therefore, is to shed light on the dark side of wealth to enlighten the intellectually curious while offering healing to the objects of their curiosity—in the hope that this awareness and understanding will bring compassion.

A favorite fantasy for those who aren't wealthy is what their lives would be like if they *were*. Certainly, it's not hard to see that being able to pay the bills and, beyond that, being able to afford all of one's material desires would seem an incredibly freeing situation. The Catch-22, however, is that there is much more to being wealthy than attaining financial ease, and this "much more" bears its own price. For some, that price is deceptively huge.

Financial abundance typically encompasses time-consuming decisions regarding investments, legal entities, philanthropy, relationships, and work, to name a few concerns. Yes, these decisions can be handled well, but not without considerable time and effort. For instance, let's look at an apparently straightforward example. Let's say you receive a fortune, clearly more than you could possibly ever need for your own expenses. Soon, your very bright, motivated, and deserving best friend asks you to foot the bill for the education he has always coveted.

You must decide how to answer this request. You could just say no, and then you would have to decide how to handle your feelings—perhaps of guilt, selfishness, or callousness—and their effect on the relationship with your friend. Or you could say yes, and then you would have to decide *how* to foot the bill. Is it a gift? Is it a loan? Is it a loan that turns into a gift after a certain period of time? After how long? What will be best for your friendship? Is the relationship the most important element of your decision?

The challenge is to handle many complicated decisions well— very complex choices that nothing in this society has prepared us for. Otherwise you will end up psychologically running, hiding, or feeling isolated.

Furthermore, far from buying happiness and contentment, money tends to exacerbate rather than end "the heartache and the thousand natural shocks that flesh is heir to," in Shakespeare's immortal words, particularly in our society where money is often a steadfast end rather than a necessary means—and, for many, even a religion.

"To the extent that the delight in money becomes a transcendent faith," points out Lewis H. Lapham in his outspoken, irreverent book, *Money and Class in America*, "the converts to 'the world's leading religion' imagine that money stands as surrogate for all the other denominations of human currency—for love, work, art, play, and thought. Believing that they can buy the future and make time stand still, the faithful fall victim to a nameless and stupefying dread."

This book's focus, therefore, is not on the illusory delights that money can buy but on the hard work and tough decisions required to live life fully as a wealthy person. Furthermore, it is about the excitement and fulfillment reaped by those who meet the challenges well.

Stephen, forty-five, would never be a psychotherapy client, mostly because it's unlikely he would concede his need for this kind of help. He epitomizes a large group of outwardly successful people, primarily men, many of whom constitute the "new" wealth of today, having set their financial sights high in the greed-driven years of the 1980s. They well may have targeted their lives long before then, but it was in the decades of the '80s and '90s that they achieved— and, in some cases, surpassed— their most cherished dreams of material success.

Now, as they try to ease their work loads to enjoy the rightful fruits of their labor, they typically don't feel the sense of fulfillment they expected. Nor do they understand what is missing from their lives. True to their core beliefs, they assume subconsciously that since they don't feel what they thought they would feel or should feel, obviously they need more money. Sometimes they go at it again, even harder.

Stephen is a first-generation American from a large Asian family, whom I met when we were seated next to each other at a dinner party. Although his initial conversation consisted mostly of jokes, many of them cynical, beneath the humor I detected a serious foundation riddled by ambition. As we talked, it became clear to me he was used to success, having acquired it easily. In fact, he now expected it as his proper due. It was also obvious he had decided at an early age to attain great financial rewards. His whole family had struggled their entire lives, and changing his own destiny had become an all-consuming mission.

Friendly, outgoing, attractive, and immediately engaging, Stephen had become an insurance salesman and excelled at it. His *annual income after taxes, he proudly revealed, exceeded $200,000, which he now maintained by working only half-time. He had married late, he told me, had two young children, and bragged that their life together was going to be "perfect."*

He intended to make sure his children had everything they ever needed or wanted. When I asked him whether he was worried they would become spoiled, he nonchalantly dismissed my concern, and I remember thinking to myself, "He's going to give them every material thing he didn't have himself at an early age. He believes that's all he has to do to make them happy. Doesn't he see the trouble ahead?" But plainly he didn't.

Stephen complained about not having people to play golf with now that he'd worked his way up to where he had plenty of weekday time to indulge his favorite sport. It was frustrating, he remarked, and didn't seem fair. I also gathered from observing his wife that he had married "up," and I wondered if he hadn't also used his friends and relations to further his career.

Listening to him, I was tempted to ask why he didn't play golf with his wife, since she didn't work and would—happily, maybe—be available. Or why he didn't share his ample leisure time with his children. I wondered, instead, about the intimacy—or lack of it—in his marriage. Talking with Stephen, my sense of him was that of a frustrated, lost person, confused that his easy financial success didn't automatically bring him happiness and contentment as well but had led him instead to emotional poverty.

Professional observations: *Stephen is a prime example of successful business people who have plainly "arrived," but at a place that is dismayingly empty. This void, he must bring himself to realize, cannot be filled by all the money in the world—but instead with love, spirituality, and emotional intimacy. Many people like Stephen haven't* *felt the need to examine their values, priorities, or attitudes. Or to look inside themselves for the fulfillment they desire and think they richly deserve. Increasingly dissatisfied and lonely, they haven't yet realized that their answers lie in spiritual—not physical—attainments and in improving the quality of their daily lives with those closest to them. Stephen is creating a legacy for his children which reaches far beyond money. If he is fortunate, he will become concerned about the entire scope of his children's inheritance.*

If not, he will plunge them into the dark side of wealth.

This book's caution, then, is about the impoverishment of the human spirit that material riches can bring, for no one gets a free ride through life, particularly those who believe they deserve one simply because they have the price of a ticket.

"Life is difficult," M. Scott Peck makes eminently clear in his monumental best-seller, *The Road Less Traveled.* These are the book's opening words and its guiding premise. Life *is* a series of emotional and spiritual challenges, Dr. Peck assures us, and enlightened discipline—not more money—is our basic tool for coping with its problems and achieving our happiness and fulfillment.

The bottom line is that we're all dealt a hand of cards at birth. Our success in life is based on how we play those cards, not on the number of chips we're given to play them.

Because I'm an inheritor myself, with many friends and acquaintances—including most of my clients—who are inheritors as well, I have collected a fair amount of firsthand knowledge about the benefits

This book's caution, then, is about the impoverishment of the human spirit that material riches can bring, for no one gets a free ride through life, particularly those who believe they deserve one simply because they have the price of a ticket.

and pitfalls of wealth, its bounties, its perils, and its luxuries, and the silken threads of tyranny those seductive luxuries can weave. What's more, I've discovered there are few resources for people who have experienced the dark side of wealth. Their problems are invisible to most of the professional community, their challenges unacknowledged by society at large, their pains and difficulties untended by the normal systems that comfort those who are born in other circumstances. This is curious because our affluent society is turning people over to this emotional limbo with incredible speed and abandoning them in this place where fulfillment is said to be abundant yet is almost impossible to find.

Approaching the meridian of my life, I contemplated my own hellish journey to the dark side and back, accepting that the trip down had been entirely of my own making, with Satan, no doubt, right there, cheering me on.

I grew up in an environment of affluence, so I have an intimate, firsthand knowledge of the issues explored in this book. Again, though they might seem ludicrous to some, I assure you the challenges are quite real and can be painful to inheritors, for whom I bear much compassion and admiration for confronting their endemic challenges.

Before writing this book, however, I first had to sort through my reasons for wanting to do so. What were my real motivations? What could I hope to accomplish? Well, my own healing, for one thing. Approaching the meridian of my life, I contemplated my own hellish journey to the dark side and back, accepting that the trip down had been entirely of my own making, with Satan, no doubt, right there, cheering me on.

The destructive choices I made were of my own free will, but so were the restorative decisions I made on the arduous journey back, eased by the compassionate friends and professional healers who came into my life and helped me make it infinitely better. The real recovery began when I embraced my spirituality, when I realized the critical need to nurture my relationship with God if I was to right myself and achieve the strong, positive life I wanted.

I stumbled seriously at times, particularly in the early going, falling often, sometimes sliding backwards, before picking myself up to recontinue the dogged journey. Always, though, there was the certainty that I would succeed, born of the awareness that I had to lead my life according to God's will if I was going to become the person I desperately wanted to be. Since then, the healing has been remarkable, consisting of a recovery I wanted to fully fathom and offer to others in their own struggles. Since I was able to make this journey, others can too. I believe this with all my heart.

I hope to bequeath some of what I've learned and to nurture, counsel, and guide others on their own paths out of the darkness. I can't imagine a greater privilege than the work I do, to be trusted enough to be allowed into the deepest recesses of people's hearts and psyches, to be able to help facilitate their most cherished hopes and dreams.

For those of you who doubt you can achieve the same faith that I did or call on your relationship with your own god, it is important to think about what the word *god* means. Each of us has a god, whether or not we acknowledge it, whether or not we can name it. It is simply who or what you value most in life. What do you think about when making any important decision? What is your greatest resource? Is it money, family, or control? Is it the God of the Bible, the Torah, or another spiritual tradition? Whatever you find as the biggest presence when you search your life, there you will find your god.

Each of us has a god, whether or not we acknowledge it, whether or not we can name It. It is simply who or what you value most in life.

11

And although I remind myself often that I am a psychotherapist, not a spiritual teacher, I remain steadfast in my belief that a strong, healthy spiritual life is of vital importance and that the greatest challenge of wealth is spiritual.

⌐

I want to say, too, that I don't think money is either good or bad. It is a resource, like any other, which we can use for the attainment of our personal goals. It is simply neutral, possessing no moral value whatsoever. Yet in our highly materialistic society, many people ascribe morality to money, and most, certainly, to wealth. Material riches present us with a unique spiritual challenge: that we distinguish moral values from money—and recognize that, in and of itself, money is neutral in nature. Whether money is "good" or "bad" depends on the purpose for which the user is engaging it.

To see how great that challenge is, one need look no further than the Bible. In Matthew 19, verses 23–24, Jesus cautions, "Truly I say to you, it is hard for a rich person to enter the kingdom of heaven," and then he immediately stresses, "And again I say to you, it is easier for a camel to go through the eye of a needle than for a rich person to enter the kingdom of God."

Reading these verses for the first time as an adult, having acquired precious little maturity by then, I was terribly disheartened. "A *camel* through the eye of a *needle*! How could that be possible?" I asked myself dejectedly. As I read on, however, I saw that Jesus promptly assured his disciples, who were as astonished by his words as I

> **"It is easier for a camel to go through the eye of a needle, than for a rich person to enter the kingdom of God.... but with God all things are possible."**
>
> —Matthew 19:24–26

was, "... but with God all things are possible" (Matthew 19:26). This last phrase is the key to Jesus' teaching here. His disciples and I were dwelling on the letter, not the spirit, of the law. Jesus was talking about what happens when you focus on temporal wealth rather than on treasure in Heaven.

Later, in John 3:16, I read, "For God so loved the world that He gave His only begotten Son, that *whoever believes in Him* should not perish, but have eternal life" (italics mine). I realized then that I would not be excluded from the kingdom of God purely because of my inherited wealth but in fact *included* on the basis of my faith. Yet how could I make sense of Jesus' extreme caution in the earlier passage? My own spiritual challenge began with the resolve to learn where those startling words in Matthew could lead me. How could I become the person God intended despite the financial wealth bestowed on me?

Like most inheritors, I have been presented with an unusual opportunity in life. On the one hand, I have the financial ease to apply myself to being receptive to God's will for me, to act in the ways God directs me. On the other hand, I also have the financial ease to be very self-indulgent. God gives me a lot of choices. By making the right ones, I can truly honor God. I can contribute something large or small to society. This is the opportunity that wealth provides. It is the same for all inheritors. Recognizing this opportunity is the first step away from the dark side toward personal fulfillment.

How, you might ask, did I decide on the specialization of my work? Many factors came into play. Among the early ones were two attitudes about wealth that struck me forcibly, one the complete opposite of the other.

On the one hand, I was dismally impressed by more than a few elderly men and women I had encountered who possessed many millions of dollars yet seemed to be sour, unfulfilled individuals. They were convinced that virtually everyone in the world was out to get their money, including all financial and legal professionals, every fund-raising organization, as well as most relatives, strangers, and even close friends. On the whole, this was a small group of fearful, cynical, wretched malcontents.

On the one hand, I was dismally impressed by more than a few elderly men and women I had encountered who possessed many millions of dollars yet seemed to be sour, unfulfilled individuals.

I remember talking with a woman in her early forties who had recently divorced and wound up with $10 million. She was miserable and bitter over having "completely lost" her former lifestyle. She regarded her settlement as leftover change, fixating on the luxurious trips she now could not take, on the exotic vacation homes in faraway places she no longer could afford. Her Mercedes was more than a year old, she complained, and she should be replacing it with a new one, but she was afraid to spend the money. I couldn't believe how totally negative her attitude was.

On the other hand, immediately after my conversation with her, I listened to an elementary-school teacher speak to a group of around fifty parents. I knew that this man's salary was modest in the eyes of the world and that his wife wasn't employed, except "in the home" caring for their children. He had received honors for his teaching excellence, which is why he was addressing us on this occasion. In the course of the evening, he said something I will never forget.

"I have the *best* job in the world, teaching third graders," he told his captivated audience. "I absolutely cannot imagine a greater privilege or more personally rewarding work. I honestly don't know why *everyone* doesn't want to teach third grade." His face shone with delight as he spoke, and there was no mistaking the passion and fulfillment he felt.

And so I began asking myself, "What *is* wealth?" What I came up with is that *attitude* determines the answer. Attitude is the largest part of the equation in reconciling the circumstances of true wealth. Perhaps it's the whole equation.

One of the main influencers of people's attitudes is their pain. The reactions and responses to pain run the gamut, and attitudes can be built or destroyed by pain. Some of us have a low threshold for emotional pain, and often we find ourselves growing because of it.

For some people, emotional pain is ever-present and oh-so-familiar, but awareness of it is lacking. Outsiders can see the pain, and in fact, it may look to them like it would be easy for the person to just give up the pain. But sometimes when there is a great sense of entitlement and little self-discipline, the motivation to grow just isn't there. After all, the attitude of entitlement feels like a power base. This attitude often masks the pain and seems to bury the psychological discomforts behind a wall.

The problem is that since the assumption of entitlement is a false power base, it carries with it a hidden burden—hidden because what feels like power is actually hollow.

Tess came into my office to work through some very difficult issues in her family of origin. She was forty-two when I met her, and in giving me her personal history, she clearly identified the major turning point of her life. Her gratitude for this experience was evident even before she started telling the story.

She had grown up in a wealthy family where relationships were poor. She had been given a lot of opportunities, and the family had created trusts in her name. During her twenties she had a rough relationship history. In fact, it was so rough that when she was thirty-one and a friend suggested that she attend a residential program which was set up to help people get their lives on track, she decided to sign up. The location of the program was on a remote island, and the leaders were "teachers." Looking back on the experience, she realized that these teachers were actually skilled therapists—even though they didn't call themselves therapists—and that she had been blessed with their commitment to help others and with the talent and skills they had to offer.

Within a week of arriving, she was in a session with her "Basic" group when her teacher, Barry, in response to a comment she made, said, "You are an ingrate. You are a spoiled brat. And until you give up those attitudes, you will not have the life you want." She was stunned. He had said it with such love, strength, and truth that she knew he was right. She felt the tears welling up and could hardly hold herself together for the rest of that session. She made it back to her cabin and sat and cried on the front step and then cried for two more days. The tears, she explained to me, were tears of despair and fear. Tess knew that Barry was right about her ungrateful attitudes and spoiled-brat behaviors, but she was used to being who she was— she didn't know how to be any other way.

She had the fear that things had *to be the way they were in her life. Being from a well-known prominent family, she was used to people being deferential to her. She was used to having the best seats at every performance, a brand-new car whenever she wanted one, and others paying her way just because they were so honored to be with her. She had an awareness of being on top socially and felt that this was where she belonged. The question she struggled with was, "If*

I didn't have to have everything the best and the way I want it, wouldn't that mean I would be a loser?" She felt terrified to give up any of her "rights."

After letting her think about it for two days, Barry walked up to her cabin and sat down on the step beside her. He said, "So, how're you doing?" Tess answered, "I feel bad." Barry—whose nickname, she later found out, was "Bottom Line Barry"—said, "Are you ready to work?" She said, "Well, I don't know..." Barry stood up to leave, and seeing that, she added, "No, wait!" He stopped and turned around, so she continued, "It's just that if I give up who I have been, I don't know who I'll be." He said, "Right, that's your fear. I know who you'll be. You'll be that beautiful person you've kept locked up inside of you." Tess knew that again he was right, and she found the courage to say, "OK, I'm ready to work." She stayed for four months, worked harder than she had worked in her life on anything, and made it all the way through the "Advanced" group.

Professional observations: *Most people who are allowed to grow up without gratitude, appreciation, and humility have little if any awareness of their attitudes and behaviors. It is unusual for an inheritor to acquire that awareness and have the motivation and the self-discipline to give up destructive attitudes. It happens when the person gets into more pain than he or she is willing to live with. Tess was fortunate that she found great guidance and support in giving up ingratitude and bratty behaviors, and she was able to begin the wonderful journey of becoming the person she had always known secretly was there inside of her.*

Sometimes I asked myself, "When do people finally decide to change, to *truly* change?" The answer to this question strikes me as simple: *pain.* We change because we get into more pain than we are willing to tolerate any longer.

"When do people finally decide to change, to *truly* change?" We change because we get into more pain than we are willing to tolerate any longer.

It's obvious when you think about it. Our intellectual understanding of the behaviors and attitudes we would like to acquire comes to us relatively quickly and easily. The courage, however, to act on that understanding doesn't come as readily—because it's hard work to find the courage, and the work itself is painful. This is why, even when we can use our intellects to clearly envision the benefits of decisive change and fresh courses of action, it may take us considerably longer to gather the will, motivation, and self-discipline to enact those bold changes.

Like wealth itself, pain is also relative. Tess had a sensitivity and awareness that brought her to the threshold of more pain than she was willing to tolerate any longer. Pain works in different ways in each individual's life. In the following story, Amy's, Claudia's, and Kevin's experiences with pain and their responses to those experiences are all very different from each other.

I first met Amy when she was in her twenties. She came into my office at the urging of a friend. She longed for a settled and fairly traditional life with a family of her own, but so far she had found this goal to be terribly elusive. We started our work with her fear of relationships, her attitude of entitlement, and a certain rudderless quality to her existence. But she faced her challenges with courage and energy. To her credit, she saw that the only way she could possibly reach her goal was through her own efforts; no one could do it for her. I became her coach.

During our work together, she met and began dating Kevin, twenty-five, a man new to Seattle, where they both lived. He immediately struck her as smart, very funny, wild and loose, great fun to be with—just her type, she thought. He also was quite wealthy, which didn't particularly impress or interest her since she herself was an inheritor of several million dollars. They were together for most of a year, during which time she discovered he was a womanizer. Naïve as Amy was, she knew she definitely wanted marriage in her future, and she broke off the relationship on the basis of his womanizing alone.

She continued to work on her relationship skills in therapy and practiced them in her life. She found a career that she loved, and this gave her more ways to practice her growing relationship skills. Well on her way, she decided that she had reached her goals in therapy, and we ended our work.

Several years later, after having married and started a family, she came back to me. She had been asked to join the Art Museum board, and since art was related to her work, she felt complimented and was delighted to accept. During the intervening years, Amy had brought herself into a straight-and-narrow lifestyle, motivated by her vision of the kind of marriage and family she wanted. Much to her surprise, the first person she saw as she walked into the room for her first board meeting was Kevin.

When Kevin saw Amy, he greeted her warmly, since they had parted on amicable terms. At about the time of Amy's marriage, Kevin had married Claudia. He told Amy that he and Claudia had dated for two years before their marriage. Amy wondered about this marriage but hoped that, like her, Kevin had found his way to values and priorities that would support marriage well.

Kevin referred to "old times" once or twice in casual conversations with her after meetings, and Amy grew to suspect that Kevin had not embraced the values needed for a successful marriage. One clue had been evident to her at the first museum event both couples *had attended. Amy's husband, Brian, had lingered at the door to check their coats when Amy, looking at the crowd, saw Kevin approaching her to say hello. As they talked animatedly, she noticed that Kevin's wife, Claudia, intruded abruptly into the conversation. "This woman is worried about her husband's connection with me," Amy thought at the time, but she shrugged off the notion because it wasn't her problem.*

It wasn't long before her doubts that her lifestyle was really quite different from Kevin's proved to be well-founded. He continued to attempt to reminisce with her about their former wild times together, and she sensed uneasily that he would overstep the boundaries of friendship if she would just unlatch the gate.

The common sense she had developed helped her set her boundaries. After telling him only that she "really didn't remember much" about their old days together, he gave up on that connection. The truth, however, was that Amy did remember much more than she cared to admit. She remembered his womanizing character, for one thing, but she simply decided to compartmentalize the past. Nor did she see any benefit that could possibly result from revealing to either Brian or Claudia the details of her bygone romance with Kevin.

Amy's refusal to revisit their years together also sent a clear message to Kevin and drew a line he knew he could not cross. She did, however, observe his and Claudia's relationship with a fair amount of interest. Amy was particularly curious about how Claudia handled the inevitable "other" women in Kevin's life.

One of the reasons Amy came back to therapy was that in spite of her clarity about her own relationships, she had become aware of moments of envy, in particular toward Claudia and the many expensive and exquisite gifts she received from Kevin. Amy knew that the work she had done in therapy was irrevocable. She could not go back, Kevin had not changed, and she liked her own marriage. But she was surprised to find that she felt envious of what looked like an abundance of gifts from Kevin to Claudia.

Eventually, as we worked on strengthening Amy's sense of her worth and her values, she found out more about the context of Claudia's gifts. They had been "I'm sorry" gifts for Kevin's affairs, Claudia disclosed. Claudia's revelation came as she was building the case for her divorce from Kevin.

"You know," she told Amy, "all the beautiful, expensive jewelry I have, even the boats, the vacations, the cars, the houses, they're all gifts he gave me to make up for screwing around with other women. I'm really disgusted by it all." In that instant, any envy Amy had ever felt for Claudia's exquisite, extravagant possessions instantly evaporated.

Professional observations: Amy clearly had developed strong and appropriate boundaries in her relationships. Even though Amy had worked hard to develop values she felt she could build her life on, she was "human," and the pull of "worldly" values is strong. The negative emotion of envy had caused Amy pain beyond her ability to cope without outside help, and the emotional pain of the occasional envy she felt was enough to motivate her to examine her life and to work through her feelings. A conscious review of chosen values and priorities is often enough to shed the emotion of envy.

Amy's story also illustrates the relative value of wealth. Despite being an inheritor herself, she had far less money than did Kevin, and yet she "felt" wealthy most of the time even though she had been tested by her envy of the luxuries lavished on Claudia by her husband.

To Amy's credit, once she discovered the context of these gifts, her envy, already fading, disappeared entirely.

Only, it seems, when our old behaviors and attitudes get us into enough pain do we become sufficiently brave, determined, and impelled to start the long journey back to the best person we can be. That journey—through the eye of the proverbial needle—is what this book is all about.

The Territory

THE EMOTIONAL TERRAIN of the work I do resembles a geographic landscape. The people who come to me with their challenges invariably have financial wealth in the background or foreground of this terrain. The challenges for which they seek help, typically, are guilt, self-esteem, relationships, motivation, self discipline, and work. The two areas where we start most often, by far, are relationships and work.

These areas are challenging for most people regardless of their economic status, but where wealth is concerned, the emotions and the choices are usually exaggerated. This, in itself, is problematic. If one mixes strong emotions, myriad choices, and diverse financial resources, it is easy to become tentative and confused. Add to this indecisiveness, no real need to sustain an earned income, and it's possible to see how the inheritor can stall out. Most inheritors don't like this stalled-out feeling, for it is human nature to want to feel productive.

One landscape of the territory to be explored is the desire to feel productive, which can be hampered, or even brought to a standstill, by the privilege of wealth. Most of us—inheritors and non-inheritors alike—need some form of work to feel a sense of fulfillment. Some are fortunate to find a vocation or job that fits them perfectly, and they never look back. This is rare, but it happens. Others—the majority of us, in fact—struggle to get the right fit.

Most people don't appreciate the sense of purpose and fulfillment that comes from work. Many resent their work because it keeps them from playing. They think they're working just to pay the bills—and if they really do hate their jobs, perhaps they *are* working solely for financial reasons.

Others feel their jobs are adequate and have never paused to reflect on the sense of fulfillment, the accomplishments, the feeling of competence they derive from their work. Some inheritors get stuck longing for this work-related gratification. Not motivated by the need for earned income, they don't have enough hunger and self-discipline to begin or sustain a career. They lack the tenacity to see their endeavors through, never achieving the sense of fulfillment for which they yearn. It is as if they are trapped by a shadow: the dark side of wealth.

Forty-year-old Sam is a would-be journalist with the talent, education, and desire to excel at his chosen profession—but none of the drive to carry it off. The crux of his problem is the family fortune he inherited at age twenty-one, providing him with more than enough money to sustain any lifestyle of his choosing.

The burr under his psychological blanket—one he can't shake—is the need to feel like a traditional breadwinner in the eyes of family and friends: the modern equivalent of the intrepid hunter foraging for game in the rigorous wilds.

Consequently, Sam has struggled all of his adult life with reconciling his lack of motivation—which carries no financial consequence because of his wealth—with his lifelong aspiration to become a successful, admired, highly paid writer. At the same time, he feels less of a man for not having achieved his long-held dream, especially since he has studied and acquired the skills to do so.

A self-proclaimed perfectionist with no tolerance for creating anything less than what he calls "the best of which I'm capable," he literally sits on the fence of life, not giving his talent the opportunity to succeed or fail on its own merits. His "jobs" to date have consisted of various "special arrangements": part-time work, only certain types of assignments subject to his approval, extended vacations mixed with long sabbaticals, and so forth.

Predictably, as a result of this highly preferential treatment, he feels "different," not one of the team, an overpaid prima donna. Bright, mentally agile, emotionally resilient, but heavily invested in staying on the fence, Sam was a difficult client in therapy. After prolonged attempts to dislodge him from his tenacious perch, what he did secure from his sessions was an extensive awareness of his entrenched position on the sidelines of life.

But this is the place he has chosen to be, regardless of the conflicting emotions he experiences. This realization and his reluctant acceptance of it were a triumph of sorts for him. He remained stuck on the sidelines but with far more awareness—and acceptance—of his ambivalent attitudes and behavior than when he started his therapy.

Professional observations: *Sam's struggle with his attitude of entitlement to "have his cake and eat it too"—the antithesis of "I owe, I owe, so off to work I go"—is a common legacy of inheritors. His case is a classic example of a cushioned life severely contesting personal, professional, and artistic promises.*

This is an area in which the inheritor faces very different challenges than the non-inheritor. Sam's case aptly illustrates why inheritors must find a way to sustain the motivation and drive to achieve a profession or career that works for them. There are many ways to accomplish this: deriving support from your spiritual practice, using a therapist for accountability and as a rudder to help guide you in your choice of action, finding a career for which you are eminently suited (work that only *you* can do), making your endeavors an example for your kids, or doing them to create balance and harmony in your marriage. Obviously, the way to support your motivation to work must be tailored to *you*.

The point here is that motivating and fulfilling work *can* be found. For an inheritor, finding it can take much dedication and effort, requiring a deliberate choice and the decision to commit to it. For non-inheritors, lack of wealth narrows the options, limiting the freedom to choose. For them, it is a case of working to live and to reduce suffering or of not working and suffering the consequences.

Sometimes, when clients first come in, feelings of guilt are foremost on their minds. "Why me?" they ask. "Why have I been given all this and others have not?" Many who don't have financial wealth might laugh at such a trifling consideration. But for many inheritors, this moral conflict over their worthiness to possess their good fortune weighs heavily on them. It might be due to their personal sensitivity or the result of low self-esteem. Only when people are secure in themselves do they feel truly worthy of their station and role in life. Also conducive to a balanced and healthy emotional life is a well-established spiritual practice—because, again, the greatest challenge of wealth is spiritual in nature. And when the challenges of self-esteem and spirituality are well-met, the inheritance fits.

Low self-esteem is often symptomatic that the inheritance does *not* fit. Some inheritors are aware of this as a problem. For others, low self-esteem is simply woven into the fabric of their thoughts and actions, obvious to the astute observer, but not at all clear to the troubled inheritors themselves. They sense, for example, but don't question the conviction that they *must* be able to spend whatever amount of money is necessary to acquire whatever it is they want. It is simply a *given* in their lives.

The word *entitlement* encompasses this reflexive feeling, for many inheritors grow up without ever hearing the admonition, "We can't afford that." The very idea of living "beyond one's means" is totally absent from their consciousness. That there *are* no means beyond which they can live becomes part of their identity. Another part of the inheritor's persona is the idea that having to consider what things cost somehow makes one less of a person. And so it can be threatening at first to consider budgeting or the radical notion of not being able to afford something, *anything*. Happiness becomes bound up with the unquestioned assurance of total financial freedom.

Part of the inheritor's persona is the idea that having to consider what things cost somehow makes one less of a person. Happiness becomes bound up with the unquestioned assurance of total financial freedom.

The irony here is that none of us can mature in terms of financial responsibility and personal development without summoning the courage to relinquish this attitude of "I can do *anything* financially. *Everything* is available to me. I don't have to lower myself by even *thinking* about money."

One of the kindest things in regard to money that my father did for me happened when I was thirty. I had two trusts back then, although I didn't know how much money was in either of them, and my dad was the trustee for both. Essentially he provided me a monthly allowance, even though we didn't call it that, and sometimes—well, often—he told me I was spending too much. It was all rather insignificant to me since I didn't know how much was in the "pot" or how my spending related to it, so I never really changed my spending habits. I tried occasionally, but since there were no consequences when I failed, it didn't really matter to me.

What I didn't realize was that it mattered to *him.*

One day he told me, "This isn't working well. I'm going to introduce you to a trust officer at the bank. He'll have access to the money from the trusts, and you'll receive your income from him, and only from him. I'll be out of the picture." I didn't like that arrangement at all, but my father could be a brick wall, and I knew this was one of those times. So we went to the bank and I met Jess Rogerson.

At first I was nervous about the change, not knowing exactly how it would affect me. The trust officer, on the other hand, was extremely pleasant and businesslike and didn't seem nervous at all. After my father left—I imagine he felt a big burden lifted at that moment—Jess said, "The first thing we need to know is how much you spend every month." Of course, I had no idea, and that's where we started.

From then on, I kept records; I made a budget; I learned to live within that budget—painful as it was since Jess wouldn't give me extra money when I ran out. It took me a year, almost two, to adapt to my new restraints—and some refinements toward the end included my getting a job—but guess what? I grew to love my self-imposed discipline. I felt financially responsible and fiscally skilled for the first time in my life. Needless to say, such a feeling provides a tremendous boost to one's self-esteem, which is vitally important to leading a productive, fulfilling life.

The vast majority of parents do the best they can for their children. Yet the very thing that affects one child in a certain way will affect another in a completely different manner. The high standards instilled in me by my parents are a case in point. For one child, a parent's attempts to inculcate high standards can have a devastating effect despite the best of intentions. This can happen when the child's experience is that of constantly having one's shortcomings criticized and corrected, coupled with a lack of encouragement and praise. It can psychologically cripple a sensitive child, plunging him into the dark side without any lifeline.

High standards, on the other hand, held up with sensitivity and compassion, with emphasis placed on reassurance and approval, can have a wonderful nurturing effect on children and parents alike. Parents in this latter group can also exemplify for others—teachers, church leaders, neighbors, friends—the enhancing ways these high standards can work. They can lead by example and inspire the parental efforts of others. A recent experience comes to mind:

When I arrived at school one afternoon, the teacher of a friend's five-year-old son had told her of a troubling incident that had occurred. Another boy's feelings, she said, had been hurt by her son's "unkind words." As soon as my friend got to a phone, she called the boy's mother to tell her she was sorry this had happened and to ask her if they could explore together how to help their two sons grow. Aware of her own high standards of behavior for her son, she was sensitive to the other mom's concern too and knew that both boys could be encouraged and helped with compassionate, practical coaching.

If, therefore, the high standards you hold up to your children are a personal priority to you, your *availability* to deal with the potential challenges they bring must be a high priority as well. The stressful times when a child's attitudes and behaviors fall short of a parent's expectations must be handled quickly and responsively. In other words, the high standards you maintain for your children cannot be aloofly imposed. They must be a constant, hands-on endeavor.

Critical, too, is that all dialogues with our children about our elevated expectations of them *must* be front-loaded with encouragement and praise. At the same time, parents need to be as attentive to their own spirituality as the lofty standards they hold up for their children. In so doing, we will assure a minimum of anxiety for ourselves in the stressful moments that will inevitably ensue.

On another personal note, while in my early thirties I was fortunate to live out one of my hopes and dreams, that of playing in a rock band. I entered this dream very much through a side door, in that the band belonged to my best friend's brother and I was in charge of producing several events that required a band. After the first performance, I brought up the idea of playing keyboards in the band myself. Everyone but me was skeptical of the arrangement, but they let me try it and everything went well.

And I *loved* it. It truly was a dream come true. But because I felt the hold on my place in the band was tenuous at best, I asked our drummer one day, "How do you make a real place for yourself in a band?" He replied: "You make a place that is yours alone, a role that only *you* can fill." So for the next three years I set up events for this group—something only I was willing to do—and thus made a real place for myself in the band—and, in fact, in *life* itself.

The moral of this story is that each of us needs to find our own place in life, to create the role that only *we* can fill. The lesson here is that each of us must figure out what that role and that place is and make it uniquely ours.

Because inheritors can buy their way into so many places and things, sometimes these harder real-world lessons never get learned. Looking back, I'm not surprised that I was thirty-five years old before I figured out that I had to make my own place in life.

Leslie, a youthful-looking forty-year-old woman, was in the midst of a divorce from Neil, her handsome, charming, and clever husband of seventeen years. When she married him, Leslie was twenty-three and her parents had pleaded with her to wait, but she was "in love," she said, and had no patience for waiting. Independently wealthy, she had been left a large part of her inheritance by her grandparents, and the money was already in her name at the time of her marriage.

Both intimidated and bored by financial discussions with her planning and legal advisors, she gladly turned over full management of her assets to her new husband. She insisted that everything be set up in joint accounts so that his easy access to their funds would facilitate whatever he felt he needed to do. Leslie was content to raise their children and enjoyed playing tennis, gardening, and volunteering for various charitable causes.

Once in a while, Neil would ask her to sign a document or two, which she always did dutifully and without question, although she occasionally joked that she could be signing her life away and wouldn't even know it. She trusted her husband and was relieved to be "taken care of." Managing a financial portfolio was complicated business, full of the ups and downs of the stock market, he told her, and she readily admitted she didn't know much about it, nor did she really care to learn.

What's more, as she revealed to me during our first session, her husband had surprised her one evening with the traumatic news that he had "found" someone else and was leaving her. Though surprised in a way, Leslie admitted she had long thought he'd been having an affair, but not wanting to rock their marital boat, she had never pressed him on her suspicions. However, after the divorce proceedings had begun, her attorney, in possession of the couple's financial statements, informed her that almost all of her inheritance of millions was gone.

Professional observations: Leslie had gotten stuck in the intimidation and boredom with which many inheritors meet the necessities of wealth. For them, there has always been plenty of money, someone has always taken care of the details, and they just won't gather the courage to tackle the tedious job of growing up financially and legally. Some inheritors, like Leslie, pay a serious price for relegating that personal responsibility. Her story is surprisingly common.

It is important to mention here that one way of looking at Leslie's painful lesson is that perhaps she needed to have the experience of losing her wealth, which doesn't have to be bad or good. Perhaps it was an essential step in the journey of her life.

Unless people come from the culture of inherited wealth, they are not at all likely to be familiar with its pitfalls and quicksand. Bits and pieces of the terrain, yes, but its entire geography, no. There can be many surprises and discomforts for outsiders who try to come in and make themselves comfortable.

Dana's best friend encouraged her to come in to see me. After twenty years of marriage, Dana had decided to divorce her husband, Jack, a very wealthy man who came from several generations of inherited wealth. She was an angry client. The main problem, she told me, was his relentless infidelity. As difficult as that sounds, the problem was actually much broader.

Dana had dated Jack for seven years before she could get him to express any interest in marriage. From Dana's point of view, she and Jack had a good relationship at first; mainly, they could always think of more ways to have fun. There was one dark theme in their relationship, though, even while they were dating: He seemed to have other girlfriends most of the time, even during the years after they moved in together. She was a beautiful, charming woman and had confidence in her attractiveness. She believed his infidelities would vanish after marriage.

Dana had come from a modest background, and her marriage to Jack, considering his vast wealth, seemed like the ultimate security. In her focus on that security, there were many factors she failed to consider, and she was completely unaware of them. They were married, the infidelities continued, and predictably, the fighting over them escalated. The couple had children, and still she clung to the belief that his behavior would change. It did not. By the time I met her, she was full of anger. Slowly it had dawned on her that she had married into a family whose culture dictated that infidelity was tolerated.

Dana said that Jack's father and grandfather had been womanizers as well. "The apple doesn't fall far from the tree," she had added caustically, and then she told me she had been subtly encouraged by Jack's family to view this trait as incidental and acceptable. This had infuriated her further. "I could never find such behavior acceptable," Dana concluded. "I could never tolerate his affairs."

Professional observations: Dana began her work as an angry client, but there was true sadness underneath. Jack's apologies and promises had become empty. Nothing he did for Dana or gave her was even a drop in the bucket needed to heal her pain. She and I had extensive exploring to do. First, we needed to find out what compelled her to marry Jack when she knew he was a womanizer. "Security" was the easy answer, but her sadness and pain were so big that the wealth did not assuage them.

She had to face the fact that she had thought wealth would fix anything, but now that she had lost her marriage and her children had lost their family, she knew that it didn't. She also had to acknowledge that she had married into a culture very different from *her own. In addition to the tolerance of infidelity—which, of course, might or might not be part of any family's culture—there was a completely different set of rules and standards she had come to know over the past twenty years.*

And then there was the attitude of entitlement. She had been unprepared for this, and at first it was not even recognizable to her. She may as well have married someone from a different race and a different country, she concluded. When she married Jack, she had honestly believed that her life was going to be perfect, and then she was really quite confounded by the imperfection of it all.

As for Jack, until his attitude of entitlement and his spoiled-brat behaviors bring him enough emotional pain to inspire him to do the tough work of personal growth, he will not be able to maintain a healthy, loving relationship. As anyone ages, significant changes of this kind are difficult and become less likely, though certainly possible. He had never received the proper guidance and training to be respectful, faithful, and considerate in his relationships, particularly with a spouse. He had not had a role model in this aspect of his life and had never been inspired to acquire the positive character traits necessary to sustain and nurture a marriage.

So he had drifted into adulthood with an attitude of entitlement, spoiled-brat behaviors, and the arrogant presumption that he could simply buy all the love he needed, whatever the cost. The result was that he had attracted and married a woman whose overwhelming picture of him was security. Now, at the age of fifty-five, the likelihood of his changing was slim. I wondered if he would ever be loved by a woman just for himself, for who he was apart from his wealth. Before marrying Jack, Dana saw only her fantasy of the culture of inherited wealth. She had no idea how extensive this culture really is, how insidious it can be, and how well-prepared she would have had to have been to handle it.

An understanding of three definitions is important as we begin our journey of discovery and learning. The first is *money*. It is helpful to look at money simply as a form of energy in our society. Every culture employs some form of currency as a means of exchange for business and professional transactions. You could view money as electricity—as merely energy to make things go, to facilitate society's exchange of goods and services, nothing more, nothing less.

You could view money as electricity—as merely energy to make things go, to facilitate society's exchange of goods and services, nothing more, nothing less.

This is an apt analogy, except that there is one important difference in how we view electricity and in how we view money. Most of us regard electricity in a neutral way, in fact, with little interest; on the other hand, most of us ascribe a *moral* value to money. We consider it to be good or bad, perhaps even good *and* bad at times.

This moral value we attach to money complicates the attitudes and emotions we bring to our understanding of this medium of exchange—attitudes and emotions that are unnecessarily complicated and that can even be destructive. If you view money simply as a form of fuel, a kind of energy that makes things move in our society, you will see that the emotions, attitudes, and behaviors that money often triggers (e.g., greed, arrogance, envy, resentment) can be a great waste of energy.

The second definition we need to consider is *wealth*. As recently as a century ago, the word encompassed health, spiritual life, family, even a good job. Today, though, the vast majority of people would define it purely in financial terms. So if we stick with today's colloquial connotations, the word usually means a *lot* of money. Furthermore, the definition is a highly personal one. Whatever "a lot of money" means to you, it is inevitably a different dollar amount than the one, say, that your neighbor, friend, or another family member would specify. Most things in life are relative, and this is surely the case when it comes to wealth.

There is no way, therefore, to standardize a definition of wealth because it is based on the many different lifestyles that members of society have chosen. An illustration of this fact could be the exemplary teacher we all have known and considered to be "wealthy" despite the modest salary he or she earns. And from that salary, this admirable person is able to put aside an amount to save and invest each year and believes that the relatively low *financial* pay for his job is compensated because of the privilege it affords to guide and inspire students.

On the other hand, we all have known not-so-admirable people with considerable financial assets who nonetheless lead lives of desperation, anger, and insecurity, fearful they will never have "enough," and who constantly ruin personal relationships with their money-related suspicion, aggressiveness, and hostility. Surely few would call these persons "wealthy."

Perhaps, then, the centuries-old definition of wealth as being non-monetary assets still prevails, albeit quietly.

This leads us to our third definition: what wealth *represents* to each of us personally. If you possessed whatever amount you deemed to be "wealth," what do you think it would bring into your life that you don't now have? Or, if you already own that wealth, what has it brought into your life? Does wealth signify power to you? Does it mean freedom, security, control, love, autonomy, happiness, fulfillment? The list varies widely from the most positive qualities imaginable to the most negative, and it is different for each individual.

Another question you might ask yourself is, "If I had wealth and all the time I needed to spend it on whatever I wanted, what would I be doing?" Your answer will reveal exactly what wealth means to you.

Caroline, the eldest sister among four siblings, all close in age, was twenty-one when I first met her. Three years earlier, her godmother had died and left her entire estate to Caroline and her sister, Margaret, eleven minutes younger and also her goddaughter. She bequeathed each of them $8 million. Their two brothers, Steve, a year younger than the girls, and Joe, a year younger than Steve, both had other godmothers and did not share in their older sisters' good fortune.

The children's parents had divorced when they were young, and the mother and her four children had remained close for many years. Though not poor but certainly not rich, their financial circumstances could have been described as modest. Needless to say, Caroline's and Margaret's inheritance had quite an impact on them all. From the moment of the godmother's generous bequest, the family's lives became an emotional roller coaster—one that eventually crashed, as far as Caroline was concerned.

All of them, at first, had been excited about the money. Both girls shared it generously, paying for cars, trips, and education expenses for everyone. Eventually, though, the conflicts emerged as the family members' values were challenged. One brother's education fund, for example, was dissipated through ill-advised investments. After a while, the eldest daughters began to view the money as theirs, not the family's. The result was accelerated acrimony over the withdrawn generosity.

To make matters worse, Caroline and Margaret came to disagree on their perceived "responsibilities" to the family. Caroline, in

> "If I had wealth and all the time I needed to spend it on whatever I wanted, what would I be doing?" Your answer will reveal exactly what wealth means to you.

particular, felt they had squandered all their closeness and love. She cried deep, heartfelt tears during our sessions together as she struggled to achieve emotional clarity and an acceptance of what she perceived to be a personal tragedy precipitated by her inherited wealth. One incident, in particular, evidenced the bizarre twists of fate brought into her life by considerations of money.

About a year before we began her therapy, Caroline related, she had gone to her mother's home to spend a holiday. While she was there, she decided to retrieve a scrapbook she had stored in the attic. Looking around for the book, she discovered in a far corner a covered pile she'd never noticed before. Curious, she pulled back the sheet to find numerous wrapped presents—from birthdays and Christmases of years past. Reading the tags, she found they were gifts to her and her sister, Margaret, from their godmother that had been put away in the attic instead of given to the girls.

Confronted, Caroline's mother told her she had done it to spare her younger brothers the hurt they would have felt by not receiving presents of their own from the girls' godmother or from their own godmothers. Caroline told her mother she didn't understand her actions and thought there was more to her reasoning than she revealed. She came away feeling she didn't receive all the information she needed to make sense of her mother's decisions, and she realized that she needed to work on reaching acceptance of the startling discovery in the attic.

Professional observations: *It would be easy to find lots of people who think that receiving an inheritance under just about any circumstance would be great. The challenges to relationships, especially when it tips the financial balance in a family so hard, can catch everyone off guard and confuse them.*

Taking Charge

ONE OF THE GREAT PRIVILEGES of my life was my friendship with Joseph Campbell. I was in my early twenties when we first met. In the midst of studying for a master's degree in English, I heard about a workshop he was giving at Esalen Institute in Big Sur, California. Fascinated with myth in literature, I went, having no idea he would show me that this fascination which I thought was intellectual was really *personal*. I was curious about the heroes he wrote of —as in his poem "The Battle": "The heroes of all time have gone before us . . ."— and it dawned on me that it is up to each of us to become the hero God intended us to be. With this introduction into his bright, new world, he became my generous and encouraging mentor.

Looking back, I imagine he inspired and led hundreds of newly awakened young adults such as me. Yet, in those golden days, I felt specially chosen, knowing he always had time for me and cared deeply about my journey. It was around the time of our first meeting that I began to understand that it was up to me— and me alone—to play the hand of cards I had been dealt at birth and that it was within my power to find the way to do it wisely.

⁓

Things will not make us happy. This wisdom is as old as the hills, but we need to constantly revisit it because we all forget at times what is most important in our lives. A recurrent temptation is the belief that material possessions will bring us the happiness we desire, and understandably so, because they do give us a *taste* of happiness. This taste, however, though superficial and short-lived, is revered in our society because it is a "quick fix," perfectly tailored for the impatient, and because it is decoratively evident, for many of the values common to our society are based solely on appearances.

Nonetheless, the slivers of happiness we derive from acquiring possessions—a new house or a new car or new clothes—are touted everywhere in the media. They are lauded by friends and ultimately believed by most of us to be the objectives that bring us joy and fulfillment, and we pursue them relentlessly. ("When the going gets tough, the tough go shopping.")

However, anyone who gathers the courage to reflect honestly on this pursuit of material abundance will admit that it never brings deep or lasting happiness. True happiness comes only from a profound sense of purpose and from nurturing relationships with others, particularly our relationship with God.

It is also important to acknowledge that everything has a *cost*. If you choose to pursue the "almighty buck," there is a cost that comes with it. If, instead, you choose to follow Jesus, there will be a different cost, but a cost nonetheless (Matthew 8:19–22). If your aim is to achieve excellence in a sport, there is another cost. Meaningful relationships with family and friends bring yet another cost. Whatever your choice, there is always a cost.

That is why it is imperative for each of us to know our values so that we can consciously base our priorities on those values. To acquire true happiness and lasting peace of mind, we must be aware of exactly what we are *choosing to pay for* in life and how much it *costs* us. Then we base our actions on our priorities. If we take responsibility for choosing carefully and act with self-discipline, we will not be compromising our values. If we do *not* choose carefully and instead act on priorities that are based on our unconscious values, we will be on the surest path to stress. Many people live their lives going against the grain of their true selves, going along with the crowd, not standing up for what they believe in. The courage it takes to become aware of your values and to act on them is one of the best stress-management techniques there is.

Kate and her husband, both in their mid-thirties, were clients who made a strong, positive effort to be good parents, a challenge they had found difficult in some ways in their wealthy world. Kate came into my office one day with a story of disappointment and frustration. She and her sister, Lizzie, and their respective children had been invited by their mother for a swim and lunch at the family's beautiful, exclusive country club, where she and Lizzie were members as well.

She, her ten-year-old daughter, Megan, and her six-year-old son, Carl, had come on time for the 11 A.M. swim, Kate related. Lizzie, however, and her six-year-old daughter, Jordan, had arrived an hour and a half late. What's more, they had brought a puppy into the club with them, clearly an infringement of the rules, as Kate was certain Lizzie knew because none of them had ever seen a dog inside the club.

Her sister's behavior hadn't surprised her, Kate said: "It's something you'd almost expect her to do." What did disappoint and frustrate her, she pointed out, was being put in the position of having to explain to her children that breaking rules to which one has agreed to abide is wrong. Also, because the unacceptable behavior—tardiness as well as a blatant disregard for authority—had been her own sister's, Kate's irritation had been keenly felt.

What made it even worse for her was that Lizzie had blithely excused her inappropriate actions with an account of their mischievousness in "smuggling" the puppy into the club by "hiding" it from the waiters. "Besides," Lizzie rationalized, "people don't really mind because he is so cute," and then she went on to relate how she had come to purchase the puppy. She had allowed Jordan to browse in a pet shop, Lizzie said, while she shopped for groceries next door. Jordan had then come into the grocery store, pleading for her to come right over and look at this cute puppy. "I didn't want to go," Lizzie said, "because I knew that if I did, I would have to buy the puppy."

"I would have to buy the puppy!" Kate repeated her sister's words to me in exasperation, going on to say that the incident had made her grieve once more, as she had done many times in the past, over the shared values she and her sister could have had but didn't. Kate told me she felt right in not excusing her sister's behavior at the club, using the incident instead to teach her children that rules do, in fact, apply to everyone without exception and that their aunt's attitude of entitlement—"The rules are for everyone else, not me"—was inappropriate behavior. In conclusion, Kate wondered aloud if Lizzie was even aware she had inflicted a negative influence on her own daughter by example. Jordan, she said, had bragged that the family owned five dogs now. Kate wondered if even one was perhaps too many.

Professional observations: *One of the pitfalls in choosing the "high road" of life is that those who make this choice can come into conflict with family members who drift with poor boundaries. Kate longed for affirmation and support from the people from whom it could have come naturally—her own family. Instead, their behavior often had the potential to negatively influence her children. These examples of disrespect, entitlement, and poor boundaries were a continuing source of disappointment for her. She knew better than* *to expect her sister to change, but being with her was work. Part of the work for inheritors taking the "high road" is resisting the pull of their family of origin to embrace negative behaviors that are more the norm in the family.*

One of the ways to begin introducing control into your life is by thinking about what constitutes *real* versus *imaginary* control. The two are quite different, indeed. Ask yourself what you actually control and what you only imagine you control but, in reality, don't.

For instance, you can control your activities during a holiday or your exercise regimen for a given week, but you cannot control the attitudes and behaviors of your siblings. You can control whether or not you write a will and what it says. You cannot control your father's willingness to talk with you about sports but not about investments.

The sooner, therefore, that you accept what you can and can't control in your life, the better off you will be. By continuing to lust after control you can never have, you will remain immature and constantly frustrated. There is also the question of what control others have over you. How much real control are you letting someone else have? How much of your freedom is imaginary?

Twenty-five-hundred years ago, Aesop told this fable:

A lean, half starved Wolf was walking around in the moon-light one night with his ribs almost sticking through his skin. He happened to meet a fat, happy Dog who looked very pleased with himself. After they had said polite How-do-you-do's to each other, the Wolf asked the Dog if he would mind his asking a question.

"Will you please tell me why you should be so much better off than I am? I don't mean to be rude, but I take

many more chances than you do, and yet you are fat and sleek while I go around almost ready to drop from hunger."

The Dog said, "You could live just as well as I, if you would do what I do."

"What's that?" said the Wolf.

"Why, I just guard my master's house at night and keep the thieves away."

"That sounds easy enough," said the Wolf, "and if I can have good food, a warm bed, and a roof over my head instead of rain, snow and very, very sketchy meals the way I have now, it sounds like the job for me. Let's go."

"Very true," replied the Dog, "just follow me," and they went off together.

While they were trotting along the Wolf happened to notice a crease in the Dog's neck and, being curious, he said, "Dog, what's that crease in your neck, how did you ever get that?"

"Oh, that's nothing," said the Dog.

"But," said the Wolf, "I want to know how you got it."

"Well, if you must know," said the Dog, "they tie me up in the daytime because I am a little bit fierce and they are afraid I might bite somebody. They let me go free only at night. In that way, they make sure that I get plenty of sleep in the daytime and I can watch better at night. As soon as it's dark they turn me loose and my master brings me plates of bones from the table himself and I am allowed to go where I want to. Pretty nice, isn't it? Come on, let's hurry up and get you a job just like it. What's the matter, why are you stopping?"

"Thank you very much," said the Wolf, "I thought there must be a catch somewhere.

"You are satisfied to remain tied up all day, without being able to do what you want at any time, and all because your master brings you some bones at night and lets you run around at a time when it pleases him.

"You think it does not matter that you are not able to do what you want when you want to do it, so long as you get enough to eat; and you pity me because I sometimes want for food. It is only keeping your stomach so full which prevents your mind from working.

"Well, you can just keep your nice, fat happiness, I'll take my skinny old freedom any day or night. I'd rather be free than fat. Liberty is what I want and what you offer cannot take its place. Goodbye."

And off he went.

The Point: Freedom is worth whatever price we have to pay for it.

Heather, who became my client when she was in her early twenties, had moved to Portland, Oregon, from another city across the country mainly because she craved freedom from her wealthy family. Although she liked living in Portland, she told me, she felt like a ship without a rudder. And though she had made friends at the drawing and painting classes she had taken at the Oregon College of Art and Craft, she had grown socially uncomfortable with these new friends because none of them had much money while she always did. (Her family accountant sent her a check every month.)

Heather thought about getting a job, partly to experience a "normal" life and partly to have more in common with her friends. When she informed her father of her plans, however, he told her, "Oh, no, don't do that! We'd have to pay more in taxes than the money you'd earn." So she had abandoned her idea of finding a job.

Heather also had some disheartening experiences with her friends in regard to the vast difference in their incomes and her lack of skills in handling those differences. One day, for example, she and a friend, Courtney, had been shopping in a trendy boutique where they saw a skirt they both loved. Each tried it on, and because the two were about the same size, the garment fit them both. Courtney, however, couldn't afford the skirt, and because Heather felt uncomfortable buying it for herself, knowing how hard her friend worked for the little money she had and how easily her own money came to her, the two left the store.

Try as she did, however, Heather could not forget about the skirt. She returned the next day to buy the garment despite her uncertainty she would even enjoy wearing it because of her lingering guilt. It was that guilt—and other such experiences—which brought her in to work with me. Although Heather is making progress, she is only beginning to resolve her money-related issues. Despite being physically distant from her family and supposedly living her own life, she is still very much controlled by her strong financial ties to her father.

Professional observations: *It is not uncommon for inheritors to crave the experience of living in a new city and escaping the name recognition they have grown up with. Some even change their names. Though Heather was on the track of taking control of her life, she was stumbling. To her credit, she was exploring what to keep and what to give up. Her sincerity and energy are great strengths for her journey.*

Freedom can, indeed, be an elusive goal for inheritors who have experienced the dark side of wealth because it must be reconciled with the genuine love we feel for those who hold the purse strings. And it has to be sorted out from the behavioral requirements, spoken and unspoken, ingrained in us by relatives and by society. Sometimes, as well, there are consequences to pay—such as the wolf's hungry stomach in Aesop's fable.

Yet the rewards can make the determination and effort exceedingly worthwhile. I once knew a man who exemplifies my point. He walked away from a large inheritance in favor of freedom and never looked back. Although his subsequent income proved modest, he succeeded in living exactly the life he wanted, never regretting his choice. He isn't aware that I know the circumstances of his economic sacrifice in quest of personal fulfillment, because someone else told me. Individuals such as him generally don't talk about the path they have chosen. For obvious reasons, they are not my clients.

Naturally, I found his story interesting and well worth the retelling, though in this land of the free and the brave, I imagine that a number of courageous souls have embarked on similar journeys.

Aesop told another fable:

One beautiful morning in a mountain village, an old man and his young son set off to the market town in the valley to sell a donkey. They had carefully brushed and groomed the donkey, and they walked happily down the steep path. Soon they passed a group of people sitting by the side of the road.

"Look at those silly fools!" said one of the men. "There they go, trudging along this path, when they could be riding that sure-footed beast."

Hearing this, the old man thought it made sense. So he put the boy on the back of the donkey, and they continued their trek.

Soon they passed another group of people gossiping by the side of the road.

"Look at that lazy boy! How disrespectful he is to ride while his father has to walk!" the people said.

The old man figured that they must be right, so he mounted the donkey and the boy walked.

And a short while later, they heard this: "What a selfish old man riding in comfort while the poor little boy has to try to keep up on foot!"

Again, the old man thought that they must be right, so he asked his son to climb up onto the donkey with him.

And sure enough, soon they heard more comments: "Look at those stupid fools! That poor overloaded beast will be so worn out that no one will want to buy him. Why, you'd be better off if you carried the donkey yourself."

And again, the old man thought that what these people had to say must be right. So he and his son tied the donkey's legs together, slung him over a pole, and tried desperately to carry him on their shoulders.

This was such an entertaining sight that people ran out in great crowds to laugh at the old man and his son. And the donkey didn't like either the discomfort of his bondage or the noise of the crowd. Finally, on the bridge leading into town, the donkey kicked and struggled until he broke the ropes, fell into the river, and was drowned.

And the poor old man, tired and ashamed, made his way back home, realizing that by trying to please everybody, he had pleased nobody—and he had lost his donkey in the bargain.

The lesson: You can't please everyone. If you try, you will please no one—least of all yourself.

As you become increasingly aware of the responsibility you would like to take for your life, there are many difficult decisions you may have to make. If you find, for instance, that the dynamics in your relationship with a parent create feelings of guilt in you, you may have to decide if you need to place certain boundaries on your participation in that relationship.

Another hard choice may result from your indulgence of a parent who provides you with special treats and favors, which you know are the direct result of your patronizing attention. You may decide you want that relationship to be more straightforward so you won't feel the self-recrimination for your intentional fawning. You know you must cease your childlike behavior and stop accepting the gratuitous rewards.

You also know it is delicate surgery you will have to perform, for you genuinely want to nurture the love between the two of you. Changing the dynamics of an established relationship, therefore, requires courage, and it is not for the timid. It is the journey of a hero.

Tom had become the caretaker of a mountain cabin owned and shared by his family. Ten years before I met him, his father had died, and the cabin was among the assets he had bequeathed to his wife and four children (five equal parts, one to each). The property had been a precious legacy for the old man, who had personally overseen the cabin's construction and lovingly maintained it over the years. After his death, however, his widow had no concept of the ongoing maintenance that was required or how to go about getting it done. The responsibility frightened her, and the manner in which she expressed her concern made her seem harsh and angry.

At first, whenever any of her adult children—Tom, his sister, and two brothers—planned to use the cabin, she instructed them on the maintenance chores that were required during their visits. The four children responded differently to their mother's instructions. One simply hired someone to do whatever was required; another performed the tasks himself but resented them, thinking the work excessive; another ignored his mother's requests entirely; and only Tom complied willingly and without resentment—at first.

As time passed, however, he found himself taking on more and more of the maintenance chores at the cabin to ensure they were done right and everyone was happy. Meanwhile, other family members clashed abrasively over several remodeling projects (one contractor even threatening to sue), their guest-use-of-the-house policy, and the rules governing its general upkeep (how often, for instance, the housekeeper should come in).

None of the children had needed to think of such matters while their father was alive in that he had been a benevolent patriarch, allowing them free use of the impeccably-kept vacation home, personally tending to its meticulous upkeep without soliciting any of the children's help. Meanwhile, Tom had begun to feel burdened with the responsibilities he had assumed, in particular with the blithe assumption by others that the mantle of caretaker had passed from their father solely to him.

By the time we began our sessions ten years after his father's death, the resentment and stress Tom felt over the cabin had robbed him of all the pleasures and joy once experienced during his visits there. After many unsuccessful attempts to resolve the family bickering and conflicts over the matter, he made a decision that would have been unthinkable a few years earlier: to sell his share of the property to the other inheritors. Though he had to cope with a great sense of loss and sadness, this disentanglement had become crucial to regaining his peace of mind. To add insult to injury, they were only willing to pay him less than the market-value price. His energy and strength were spent, though. With a heavy heart, he accepted the price.

Professional observations: *Some of life's steps to maturity are extremely painful. Tom was wise to remove himself from a stressful, joyless situation that he could not resolve. Sentiment is powerful. Many of us know people who hang on to a certain stock, for example, for sentimental reasons against all good sense and practicality. Similarly, Tom had "hung in there" and tried to be a part of the mountain cabin as he always had, but he reached a point where the pain had drained him. In order to have the quality of life that he cherished, he had to move on.*

Taking control of one's life in every sense, including emotional, financial, and legal concerns, is one of the most difficult moves many inheritors make. It is a building block, though, and without it, precious maturity cannot be reached.

It is an important step out of the dark side of wealth.

CHAPTER FOUR

The Importance of Relationships

A CONCERN OVER RELATIONSHIPS is what brings most of my clients in to see me. It is a huge subject for inheritors, as it is for everyone else, because of the expansive quality that relationships bring into our lives and because of the diverse number of relationships that consume us and vie for our attention. Among them are the relationship we have with God; the relationship we have with ourselves (also known as self-esteem); the relationship we have with our wealth; the relationships we have with our parents, siblings, spouses, children, friends, co-workers, and acquaintances, to name the main ones.

Primary among these, of course, is the relationship we have with God, and immediately after comes the one we have with ourselves. Self-esteem is a good place to start our exploration of the vital importance of relationships. Whenever I lead a workshop, I often begin with a session on relationships, opening with what I call its basics: self-esteem, trust, and communication. We must develop awareness, strengths, and skills in these areas in order to succeed in any healthy relationship.

Marlene first came to me for help with relationship issues when she was thirty-five. She longed for a primary relationship with a man and hoped to marry someday. That was seven years ago. Since then our work has been intermittent—she usually returns to see me when she's in a new relationship—but we've found she harbors an equally large challenge she needs to work on as well: her sense of purpose in the world.

Her father is the highly successful CEO of a multinational corporation, from whom she has already inherited many millions of dollars. However, she says, he keeps her in the dark about the exact nature and amount of her wealth. Marlene, incidentally, has willingly stayed in the dark so as not to rock the proverbial boat of his secretive benevolence. She, meanwhile, has pursued a meaningful career for herself by "trying out" different businesses, most of them of an altruistic nature such as the manufacture and distribution of sports wheelchairs for physically challenged individuals. But most of the ventures have been short-lived, either because she became bored or discouraged with the profits or the company mission.

Marlene's problem is that she gets her personal goals confused: carrying out her company mission, making a business profit, and impressing her father. I have tried in vain to help her develop her independence, thinking that if she lost her focus and reliance on her father's approval she could be able to achieve both a sense of purpose in her life and the marriage she wants to experience.

Though she seems motivated and works energetically in therapy, she remains emotionally dependent on her father. And despite her intellectual understanding of this strong dynamic in her life, she continues to drift in and out of commitments to her work, in and out of commitments to her relationships. She agonizes over her lack of purpose, and she is able to articulate her dilemma clearly and eloquently but unable to sustain her resolve to work her way out of it.

She seems as irresolute and vague about her spiritual life. Her heritage is Jewish, and she is loyal to her religious legacy, yet it is not a spiritual practice for her. She has identified the key to her drifting as her financial ease, made possible by the steady flow of money from her father, enabling her to live well and play to her complete satisfaction. Yet though she realizes the connection between her dependence on the money and her inability to function independently, the leap to rearrange any of this connection has been too great. Though extremely bright and seemingly receptive to my insights into her emotional challenges and the work she must do to achieve her sense of purpose and a lasting relationship, she appears to remain stuck, year after year.

Professional observations: *It will help Marlene to find work that she will do consistently. She can start with work for which she has a passion and in which she trusts her instincts. She needs to make a commitment to see her plan through to a goal and set up accountability to someone other than her father. Finding a mentor for work she loves could help her tremendously. She is on the right track in thinking that a sense of competence in her work will enhance her self-esteem.*

Most of us would define self-esteem simply as knowing and liking who we are. My own self-esteem has grown in direct proportion to my knowledge of God. I also believe that, despite the many ways there are to increase our self-esteem, a daily practice of knowing God better and drawing this spiritual connection ever closer is the best means available to us.

There are other kinds of practices as well that contribute to healthy self-esteem. One method I teach is the deliberate acknowledgment of accomplishments, large and small, in every area of our lives. The verbal description to ourselves of each of these major or minor successes is important. This needs to be a regular, deliberate practice for several months—preferably a year.

Goal-setting is another effective builder of self-esteem. Yet I hesitate to offer this technique as an option because most people need considerable coaching in its use. It is imperative to set small goals initially, goals that are specific and attainable. Most people immediately want to set objectives either too ambitious or too vague. I've found that if this method is not properly coached, it will likely have a negative effect on self-esteem. Used correctly, however, goal-setting can be a rich and rewarding endeavor. In fact, weekly goal-setting is a regular tool I use with clients. Since my objective is for the client to experience the sense of accomplishment that comes with meeting a goal, the actual content of the goal is secondary to me.

Wealthy, highly successful men usually cast large shadows as fathers. A very large shadow was central to Christopher's situation when he sought me out at the age of fifty. Having doggedly avoided therapists his entire life despite repeated entreaties by friends and relatives for him to get professional help, he finally came to me out of sheer desperation. At this critical juncture of his life, both of his businesses were failing, the investments he had made were losing money, his girlfriend was threatening to leave him, and he had already poisoned his relationship with his ex-wife and children. In effect, he was well on his way to estranging everyone in his life.

During our first session, I soon realized that he expected me to "fix" it all for him. Somehow he had gotten the impression that this is what therapists do: We fix the messes people get themselves into. My first task was to help him to see that it wasn't in my power to fix his life, that if he decided to work with me, it was he who would have to do the necessary work to make things right for himself. After convincing him of this painful fact, I could see he was more discouraged than ever.

Christopher's father, Charles, had been a phenomenally successful businessman. Born into a poor family in the East, his own father had died when he was an infant, and it had been his mother, a schoolteacher with a strong belief in education as the prerequisite to all achievements in life, who had set him squarely on the path to financial success. As Charles built his spectacularly profitable company, he married and his family flourished as well, growing eventually to include Christopher and three siblings, all of whom Charles loved dearly but from a distance as he continued to focus most of his energy and attention on corporate rather than family matters.

As is often the case, Christopher and his siblings grew up sheltered from the exigencies and concerns of the real world, totally bereft of business skills, and eventually crippled by low self-esteem and an attitude of entitlement. Understandably, Christopher entered adulthood with terrible relationship skills exacerbated by an abrasive, arrogant manner. By the time he sought my help at the age of fifty, the cumulative stresses and failures of a lifetime had brought him to the realization that whatever happiness, self-fulfillment, and business success he attained would have to be earned and were not simply his due. To his credit, Christopher applied himself to the difficult goal of doing the personal work that was necessary to make his life better.

***Professional observations:** Because he had lived his entire life in the overbearing shadow of his father, Christopher had in a way counted his father's successes as his own, including all of his father's innate talent, professional skills, capacity for hard work, personal luck, and fortuitous economic timing that contributed to those successes. Sadly, no one had ever discussed with Christopher the vital need for him to set his own standards and goals; to achieve his own triumphs; to develop his own innate gifts; to explore and pursue his own passions in art, science, business, or whatever field he chose in order to create meaningful work for himself. Gradually, however, he found his own path, one that led him to become the* *sculptor he had always secretly wanted to be. He also applied himself to learning and exercising the relationship skills he now knew were necessary to his happiness and fulfillment. He did this through careful goal-setting, hard work, and "baby steps."*

⌒

Until Bill came in to see me, he hadn't been out of his house in three years. He'd had his groceries delivered and shopped by mail and on the Internet. His personal trainer came to his house, as did his hairdresser. He had become a virtual hermit, although one who lived in self-pampered ease. His father was a billionaire who hadn't trusted anyone, and though Bill rarely saw him these days, he didn't trust anyone either.

Bill had finally ventured out of his house and into my office because he'd come to realize that his self-indulgent but solitary lifestyle had severe limitations. Our first conversation had to do with movie-making, something he hoped to do. He had spent years watching countless films, he told me, and he knew almost every line in his favorites. He was certain he would be producing a movie with Steven Spielberg someday, but his problem, he said, was that he didn't know how to connect with him.

Professional observations: *Trust is one of the three basic relationship skills, the other two being self-esteem and communication. When inheritors lack any or all of these relationship skills, willful isolation becomes a viable option in that they have the financial means to withdraw from the world rather than cope with it. It's hard and sometimes painful work to learn relationship skills as an adult, and a wealthy person can avoid doing so. There's only one problem with a gilded cage, however: It's still a cage.*

Everyone knows about trust issues. They are inherent in every relationship. In those cases where one person has wealth and the other person has less money, one question often rears its suspicious head: "Do you really like me for *me*, or are you attracted to my wealth?" This can be a lingering doubt, and resolving it can be a painstaking and delicate process of trust-building.

An analogy of looks, i.e., physical appearance, can be useful here, for a similar question can occur to a beautiful person: "Do you really like me for *me*, or are you attracted to my physical beauty?" The analogy is in having an abundance of an asset that is highly valued in our society. Once again, the answer lies in the painstaking, delicate process of trust-building. Its delicacy is rooted in the magnetism of wealth and beauty in our society, and its objective is the achievement of this necessary trust through honesty, openness, consistency, acceptance, and dependability. Trust-building occurs in all of the many small —sometimes very small—comments, responses, and reactions that are the daily fare of relationships. And once this vital trust is built, it is these selfsame qualities that will maintain it.

John, thirty-five, is from a large, very wealthy family in a small town with a much poorer population. He harbors a painful memory from the years when he and his older sister, Ellen, were teenagers. Some friends were having a party, and he and Ellen were invited. His sister was one of the few teens in town with access to a car, and she was counted on to provide the necessary transportation for others who would be going to the party. But when Ellen revealed she wouldn't have access to the family car that night, she was "uninvited" to the party.

Professional observations: *Yes, many people can relate to this kind of rejection. Since wealth is relative, such an experience is hardly unique to inheritors. The "uninvitation" would certainly have been a* *blow to Ellen's teenage self-esteem. I don't know the rest of her story, but I hope that she was able to put the meanness of her "friends" into proper perspective. I have no doubt that she went on to build more valuable friendships in her life. Fortunately, most of us develop more resilience as adults than we have as teenagers.*

～

Born into a wealthy, fashionable East Coast family whose members were all physically and fashionably exquisite to the point of storybook perfection, Emma's sin was unpardonable. She was obese. As a result, she had been banished to faraway boarding schools from the time she was twelve. At eighteen, arriving home after her graduation from high school, Emma was told of the generous trust that had been funded for her by her parents. It was a gift to her and would provide plenty of income, with only one stipulation: She could not come home again. The reason: Her family could not and would not tolerate this tarnish on their gleaming perfection.

Professional observations: *In our appearance-obsessed society, people often become enamored of physical beauty, coming to regard it as a "must-have" feature of their lives. Unfortunately, this need for decorative perfection can be exaggerated by wealth. When a family has the money to protect its outward appearances at all costs, one wonders how much pain such as Emma's is inflicted for purely superficial reasons.*

Though deeply hurt and impaired in her ability to trust, Emma resolved to make a great life for herself. A friend suggested that she enter therapy, and it proved to be the beginning of relationship-building and a career that was fulfilling to her beyond anything she had ever experienced as a child. She remained a large person, but in becoming a highly successful jewelry designer, she learned to look at both inner and outward beauty.

～

Everyone has a relationship with money, some with wealth. In either case, it is important for us to be aware of the depth and nature of these individual relationships. Money usually does not have an isolating effect on people, though wealth definitely can, and each person's emotional involvement is highly individual. In exploring her relationship with money, a client once said to me, "I think of wealth as my most reliable friend."

Learning about your own relationship with money involves asking questions such as, "How do I feel about balancing my checkbook?" "How do I decide how much I am willing to spend on something?" "How do I feel about the pay I receive for my work?" Everyone has some kind of relationship with money, and as in all relationships, the more you know about yours the better you will be able to handle it.

For those who have a relationship with wealth, getting to know that relationship well is also essential. A good way to find out what wealth means to *you* is to make a list of all the ways it influences your life, how it enters into your thoughts, and how it affects your daily decisions.

If you think about it a moment, you will find that wealth does, indeed, represent something specific to you. It represents many things to many people. Wealth to one person, for instance, represents power; to another, security; to another, freedom, and so on and so forth. A fairly small group of people, pooling the many influences that wealth represents in their lives, generates a very long list of these qualities.

In regard to one's wealth, sooner or later it occurs to most inheritors to ask themselves, "How much is enough?" The question is more important to some than it is to others. Nonetheless, the answer has far-reaching implications for everyone. Regardless of how interested in the question *you* might be, the answer could affect your self-esteem, your spirituality, your relationships, your investments, your spending, and your work, to name just a few of the areas of your life. What's more, your answer will change, and keep changing, as you mature.

Think about the question, though. Knowing the answer will help you define the direction and the boundaries of your life and how you probably will respond in given situations. Actually, each of us has already determined a figure, an optimum amount of wealth, an answer to the critical question, "How much wealth is enough for *me*?" in our subconscious mind.

For some people, a knee-jerk response might be, "As much as I can get!" or "The more, the better!" For most, however, an ideal amount is one that would provide the financial freedom desired but not a burden of attendant responsibilities, which would feel overwhelming.

On the subject of family meetings: if invited, *go*. These events may be boring, disheartening, scary; you may not enjoy them at all; they may even make you angry and upset; nonetheless, *go*. The reason is that it's important to know what's happening in your family's lives—both your family of origin and your extended family. Also, there will probably come a time when you can affect the legacy being created in your generation. This is very important.

What do you want to be remembered for in your family? Certainly not for being negligent, probably also not for being scared, sullen, or self-centered. Ask yourself: For what do I want to be remembered? Then make it happen.

Another aspect of staying in contact is to maintain proper family relationships. This is important even if you don't like the people to whom you're related. If family visits are difficult for you, make them short and formal so as to keep tight rein on your feelings and conduct.

We need to keep in mind that established family patterns, attitudes, and behaviors are powerful, so even after you resolve to be on your best behavior, it will be difficult to resist the old automatic reactions, regardless of your best intentions. Despite the personal progress and growth you have made, the old, familiar issues can suck you in once more, to your great dismay. Still, in the interest of amicable family relationships, contact is necessary, as difficult as it may be. Keep visits short and arrange for them in a neutral setting, such as a restaurant, which should help you feel better about your participation.

As for marriage, do it for *love*! We've all heard the expression, "Marry for money." Now, it may surprise you that, despite being an inheritor, I heartily discourage marriage based on financial considerations, but I strongly do. To some, the advice to marry for love may sound naïvely romantic, but if you want to bring out the best in yourself, marrying for love needs to be your main focus.

I say this despite my awareness that, for some inheritors, wealth is a central concern in marrying. Certainly, wealth brings an overpowering impetus to the mating process; it has even been called a potent aphrodisiac. To accurately determine, therefore, how your fiancé or fiancée tips the scales in this weighty issue, pay close attention to all the little clues: the daily comments, attitudes, behaviors, and choices that reveal true character.

For many of my clients, assertiveness is a weak or nonexistent skill when we start working together. They are usually not aware of this deficiency, even though they might allude to feeling "too passive," or they may admit that too many of their attempts to communicate have escalated into anger. Since assertiveness is an essential relationship tool, we often work on this issue early.

Make no mistake about it, the ability to make clear, kind, unemotional statements about a behavior toward you that you want another person to change is a powerful and important skill. Clients who commit to achieving this skill, and who work at making it a natural part of their personae, are taking a giant step in their lives.

When Lenore began working with me, she was aware that there was something troublesome about her communication style. Each week, I would ask her for a specific example of these communication problems in her relationships with others. Intelligent and highly educated, Lenore always provided an actual incident for use in her therapy.

There were examples involving her extended family, most of them having to do with a large family business in which she was a part-owner; there were examples involving neighbors, friends, and acquaintances; examples involving her professional work and her avocational interests. Somehow, despite being a very nice person,

Lenore had developed a manner of communicating with people that was antagonistic and abrasive.

Working together, we found the cause to be partly the result of growing up with a father who was a brilliant, successful businessman but not open to her opinions. He had been "practically impossible to deal with," Lenore revealed, and it became apparent that much of her anger and antagonism had developed from her fruitless attempts to establish a give-and-take relationship with him.

Partly, too, her problem was the result of growing up in a family where no one took the time to teach her kindness and gentleness in dealing with others or why this awareness and effort would be important in her adult relationships.

Happily, because of her strong mind and firm commitment to eliminate the anger and antagonism from her communication style, after regular practice and review, Lenore became successful to the point of not having to think consciously about her newly developed assertiveness skills. It became a joy for me to hear about the many affirming surprises she encountered because of her clear communication style and the newfound give-and-take in her approach to others.

Forgiveness is the single most powerful tool we have in our relationships. In many situations, however, despite being the only way to heal ourselves and move forward, forgiveness is such a difficult goal to achieve that most of us barely reach its threshold. To attain and to use forgiveness well, we first must understand what it *is*—and what it is *not*.

For one thing, forgiveness is not for the cowardly or the arrogant. It is for the courageous and for those who understand and accept the power of humility. Needless to say, there are many small offenses that everyone experiences which are not worthy of forgiveness. These need to be recognized and then forgotten. But in the case of truly wrong and unjust acts imposed on us by people whom we care about, forgiveness is the only mature way to respond. This is not to say that we become doormats for others; in fact, it may be wisest to avoid people who have shown that they are likely to hurt us, but forgiveness is still the mature response.

For all its glorious value to our character and spirituality, however, forgiveness is a sophisticated, often complicated, and painful endeavor. Also, it is usually a *process*, which means it is an act that needs to be revisited and repeated, sometimes forever. Why do it, then? Because every time a person forgives another for an unkind or unjust act, there is healing *in the one who forgives*, and the pain in the forgiver lessens. To those working on this difficult, freeing process, I recommend a wonderful book: *Forgive and Forget: Healing the Hurts You Don't Deserve*, by Lewis B. Smedes.

In his last year of high school, Ivan had decided to apply to colleges on his own, not asking for any help from Dad. In fact, he didn't want his father in on the process at all, so he kept the applications secret from him. However, awaiting notification from the colleges of his choice, Ivan relented one day and told his father to which institutions he had applied. The result was that his father picked up the phone that very day and got his son admitted to the best school of the lot. (How? A $25 million gift.) When his father called with the good news, Ivan felt devastated and furious.

Professional observations: *Most of us need, in some sense, to believe that we're earning our own way in life. Ivan's relationship with his father was already so poor at this point that he wasn't able to communicate his need to make his own way. He felt that his* *father's involvement had been overbearing, and he resented him for it. His father, in turn, thought he was helping, but he was guilty of making unwarranted assumptions. The net result was that he robbed his son of any sense of competence he might have experienced in getting into college on his own.*

Ivan contacted me after a workshop I gave because he knew he had to heal his relationship with his father before it destroyed him. He knew that, until he did this work, he would be stuck in a smokescreen of anger, perhaps for the rest of his life. For years he had regarded his relationship with his father as impossible to change and had suffered greatly from the frustration of his perceptions.

***Professional observations:** When Ivan realized finally that (1) he could do the work of forgiveness without the involvement and interaction of his father and (2) his reason for making the effort to heal the hurt he had experienced for so long was completely for his own benefit, to free himself to live the life that God intended for him, Ivan was able, after careful examination, to take on the challenge.*

Gratitude is another part of our lives that often needs to be shaped up. And this is an area in which irony may seem to enter for inheritors. After all, who *wouldn't* be grateful to receive a large inheritance? Yet many inheritors are ingrates, mired in resentment, jealousy, frustration, and fear.

Obviously, their ingratitude is practically impossible for their parents to understand—unless they, too, are inheritors and have *been* there. Therefore, those of the younger generation tend to feel very much alone because of their ingratitude. It is easy to understand, as well, why guilt, along with resentment, can enter into the equation.

An essential component of healthy relationships, then, is the emotional maturity that enables us to feel gratitude for what we have been given. This, certainly, is not the kind of gratitude that overlooks hurts or insensitivities imposed on us but which simply finds those qualities in ourselves that permit us to offer true gratitude despite those insensitivities or hurts. I emphasize, therefore, that searching for these qualities needs to be done with the *heart*.

In my own case, for instance, I have needed to acquire the insight and perspective to appreciate the energy, determination, and stamina I developed as a direct result of the circumstances of my youth. I am truly grateful for these precious qualities and how and from whom I acquired them. They have seen me through many mistakes and challenges and have led me to accomplishments and a maturity that I might not otherwise have seen.

There is an even greater reason why the development of our capacity for gratitude is essential to personal growth and contentment. By being grateful to God, and then to our parents and the special circumstances in which we have been raised, we are better able to meet the inherent challenges of our wealth, without rancor or resentment. By keeping gratitude in the forefront of our daily attitudes, we are better at meeting all challenges. "Consider it all joy, my brethren, when you encounter various trials, knowing that the testing of your faith produces endurance. And let endurance have its perfect result, that you may be perfect and complete, lacking in nothing" (James 1:2–4).

What is important, too, about the practice of forgiveness and the practice of gratitude is the ability to love the people whom God has placed in our lives, regardless of how difficult it may be to feel and express that love. But it is important because God has commanded us to do so. In many cases, though, this is not the warm, fuzzy love that causes us to relax and let down our defenses.

Experiences of warm, fuzzy, easy love are the restorative oases God provides us in our journey through life. The other kind of love is different. It is tough, responsible, obedient, maturing love. Once you understand and accept this difference and develop some skills in loving the difficult people in your life, this tough love can be as rewarding as the easy love, even though we need to be careful while experiencing the former, maintaining constant vigilance and awareness—protecting ourselves in the clinches, so to speak.

A unique challenge for inheritors in the area of love involves the tendency to quit when the going gets tough, instead of sticking out the rough times in a marriage, for instance. While still in my early thirties, I was married and divorced three times in six years. I barely got out of the starting gate with any of those marriages. Certainly, I never gave any of them a chance. Yet all three men were fine people. In retrospect, I realize my marital failures had nothing to do with the men I married. In each instance, I just got scared and took off like a rabbit.

Would I have been more likely to face my fears and hold my ground had there been financial constraints and repercussions? Maybe. Now that I'm blessed with a wonderful marriage that has lasted many years and rewarded my courage with maturity and precious children, I sometimes look back and wonder if I could have handled my earlier fear and immaturity in a less destructive manner.

Three good men and their families were hurt deeply by my immature attitudes and behaviors. I can't change that now. All I can do is acknowledge what I did and ask for my own forgiveness. My husband has taught me how to love, and with the understanding I have gained I can nurture our marriage and teach our children, in turn, how to love. Partly because of my wonderful family, partly because of the destructive immaturity of my past, the appreciation for what I now have is tremendous and undying. There is nothing like having to wait long and hard for something to feel enormous appreciation for it.

I have met inheritors who have arrived at the conclusion that they can only protect themselves financially by marrying those who possess as much wealth as they do. While this may make sense at first glance, one irony of this reasoning is that it limits one's choices terribly, for at once there are only a few people who qualify as desirable prospects. Suddenly, too, a great many variables are introduced. One small problem is that it is practically impossible to match your wealth equally with the wealth of a potential partner. Besides this, how on earth do you bring up such a private subject before you even know if you like each other very much?

Indeed, inheritors create a slippery slope to climb when they make wealth the key consideration in their search for a partner. Aside from narrowing the field considerably, they introduce the shallowest of qualifications into their quest for marital bliss. If a marriage is to be built on such a limiting quality, the odds grow exponentially that neither partner will experience the rich intimacy and personal growth that marriage can offer.

Many inheritors are painfully ambivalent about loans and gifts, particularly when these generous gestures concern friends whose financial circumstances vary widely from their own. In cases where inheritors are financially better off than their friends, which is often the norm, a vague uneasiness can exist that the ones with wealth will be asked to pay on all occasions simply because they possess the money. In these circumstances, too, the guilt over having much more than others often resurfaces. For these reasons and others, attempting to sort out one's values on the spot in regard to loans and gifts can become painful and distracting.

Kristin, an inheritor, turned a potentially damaging experience into an uplifting one when a friend asked her for a loan. Kristin felt her friend had a real and respectable need for the money and sincerely wanted to help her, so she made the loan. Kristin had only one stipulation: It had to be repaid within a year. However, if her friend was unable to do so within that time, then the money would become a gift.

As it turned out, a portion of the loan did turn into a gift because the friend was unable to pay the money back fully, despite her genuine attempt to do so. However, because of the way Kristin handled the situation, years later the two women are still good friends, and the gift has become a non-issue between them. In short, Kristin was able to help her friend yet not allow her kindness to affect their feelings for each other. As a result, their friendship, much more precious to Kristin than the money, was preserved.

Professional observations: *The key is in developing your awareness of your values before the fact, lining up your actions with your values and being in control of your response. Kristin had thought enough about loans between friends to see the potential danger in them. She had also decided beforehand how she would react to such a request, and she wisely decided to treat the loan as a gift. She respected her friend's desire that the money be considered a loan, and she put a* *time limit on its repayment. She knew there was a good chance her friend would not be able to repay the loan entirely, so she protected their friendship by turning it into a gift after a year. Thus, Kristin made the potential challenge to their friendship a non-issue.*

If you decide, therefore, that you want to make a gift or loan to a friend, first examine your priorities and values to see exactly how you feel about your altruism in regard to that person. Also, bring to mind the circumstances under which you would make such a loan, i.e., the types of purchases or services you would be willing to fund. Finally, ask yourself how you would feel about writing off the loan as a gift to a deserving friend.

You may need to acknowledge to yourself that your friend has, indeed, asked for a loan and not a gift and that if the friend wants to consider the money as a loan, this is perfectly all right with you. Consider telling your friend, however, that your friendship is more important to you than the money and that, after a specified time, should the entire amount still be unpaid, the "loan" will become a gift as far as you are concerned. This will preserve your friendship, as it did Kristin's, by keeping it free and clear of money encumbrances. It will keep the dark side at bay.

A clever person came up with a "Golden Rule" for inheritors. Actually, it is one that applies to all wealthy people: *He who has the gold makes the rules.* A nasty thought, granted, but if you have ever been in a close relationship involving a great disparity in the "gold" possessed by both parties, you will readily see the truth in the maxim. There are exceptions, however. They consist of those humble, generous individuals who refuse to wield their power, despite the circumstances. Most of the time, however, the one with the money callously, and sometimes thoughtlessly, makes the rules.

When an inheritor, therefore, is sensitive to the imbalance of power in a friendship and makes a conscious effort to offset or nullify it before the relationship is harmed, the result can be interesting and enriching. As both people in the relationship become more open and honest about their perception and awareness of the dynamics of power between them, they can become closer.

Douglas, a thirty-seven-year-old inheritor, has set up a trust fund for his wife. The amount of money and the conditions in the trust are generous and loving. Douglas's intention in arranging it was to equalize the power in their relationship in meaningful ways. Paramount among them is the feeling of strength Douglas's wife now feels because of the financial independence he has given her.

Professional observations: *This is an unusual act of generosity, and Douglas is wise beyond his years. He feels great about the gift to his wife because he is taking good care of his relationship with her. He is loving her in an unusual way that is available to him, and it was all his own idea.*

The emotions of people in relationships where one or both have inherited wealth are the same range of emotions experienced by those who do not have wealth to pose potential problems. A fact of life, however, is that human thoughts, feelings, emotions, and actions are often intensified and exaggerated by wealth. As a result, certain interactions can be played out too powerfully, to the point of severe detriment to the relationship. Interpersonal dynamics can be strongly affected and even harshly strained.

Yet it's the very same "stuff" everyone has to deal with: fear, resentment, love, jealousy, frustration, generosity, trust, caring, respect. All of these things are part of your relationships and mine and everyone else's. But make no mistake about it, wealth exaggerates and exacerbates all of these feelings, making them seem larger than life and harder to deal with. But it's all just human nature at work. Motivated inheritors *can* achieve excellent relationships despite the challenges of their wealth. And when they do, they come further out of the shadows of the dark side of wealth.

Teaching the Children

WHEN I WAS GROWING UP, my parents shielded me from our family's financial situation for carefully thought-out reasons. It was their sincere belief that what I didn't know couldn't hurt me. In other words, if, as a child, I lacked the wisdom to be quiet about our family's financial ease, not knowing anything about it could protect me from saying something that would cause others to envy me or to try to take advantage of me.

I understand their protective concern. I know it must have kept me from many potential problems. As I entered adulthood, though, the realization that I knew practically nothing about financial matters gave me some unease, and when the time came to shoulder my financial responsibilities, my ignorance seemed like a serious weakness.

Not that any huge crises or monetary losses resulted from my naïveté over such matters, but it was still an ignorance that held me back in my early adulthood and resulted, for one thing, in my slowness in getting my professional career underway. I share this with you now because financial naïveté such as mine is typical in many inheritors and often leads to late emotional development. I was tardy in other aspects of my emotional development as well, but the financial area is an easy one for me to describe.

I remember, in my early twenties and thirties, wanting to make charitable contributions to what I perceived to be worthy causes. Yet I never had *any* idea how much to give. Now I realize there are far worse problems in the world than the shortcoming I'm describing here. In fact, I find it hard not to worry that the vast majority of people who read this will accuse me of whining about nothing.

Nonetheless, it is important to examine financial naïveté as a precursor of late emotional development, and I need to stress the importance of educating children about finances and other challenges of inherited wealth. I recommend an excellent text on this subject: *Children of Paradise: Successful Parenting for Prosperous Families*, by Lee Hausner, Ph.D. Packed with sound, practical advice in this crucial area, the book is available from the author. (See the Resources in the back of this book.)

Yes, I most certainly *do* recommend teaching children about their inheritance in age-appropriate stages. This includes inform-ing them exactly what wealth is and what it isn't.

Yes, *do* teach children about their inheritance in age-appropriate stages.

What it *is*, among other things, is a great privilege and a great responsibility. What it *isn't*, among other things, is a license to be lazy or bratty or to assume an attitude of entitlement. Don't underestimate the deli-cate demands this vital education of your children will exert on you as a parent. Teaching them about wealth is as important as teaching them about sex, but inheritors typically are not taught any better about money when they're young than they're taught about sex. Probably worse.

What's more, now that sex is completely out of the closet, money has been called society's last taboo. Certainly, the inheri-tance of wealth would qualify as even a greater taboo in the sense that some consider it a secretive, almost shameful subject, in much the way sex was regarded for centuries. This is why this pivotal education of young inheritors must be tailored to each child. It must be a delicate, sustained building-block program.

Start with an allowance at an age when the child evidences *some* interest in receiving one. This allowance—a small amount of money given regularly to the child solely because he or she is a family member—should not be contingent on any conditions or tied to particular behavior. Then, begin educating the young recipient on choices for the allowance money: saving, spending, giving. Keep the instruction simple, interesting, and understandable, perhaps sharing with the child some of the choices *you* might make or choices that you do make with your money. Eventually, creative investment and philanthropic options can be introduced, as early as eight or nine years of age with some children, but usually not until ten, eleven, or twelve.

Most certainly, there should be rules in your home concerning every family member's responsibilities, such as bed-making, laundry care, and bathroom neatness. Again, these are obligations and duties children assume simply because they are family members—no one gets "paid" for them. In addition, there can be extra household chores available for any child who wishes to earn money above and beyond his or her allowance, tasks such as washing windows or vacuuming, helping to prepare for visits by guests, and so forth.

All of this is done to lay a solid foundation for teaching children about inherited wealth. They need to develop a perspective on receiving proper pay for proper work as well as a suitable outlook on money that comes without working for it.

Our ten-year-old daughter receives an allowance, and we also provide opportunities for her to earn additional money. She wrote the following essay to describe one of those opportunities.

The Lesson of the Inflatable Hammer

Every year in June some of my friends and our families get together in one of our driveways and have a garage sale. It's all kid stuff and the kids get to keep the money we make. At our last sale, I made one deal in particular that turned out to be great.

All day my friend, David, had been trying to sell a plastic "blow-up" toy hammer. Some of our best sales are to each other, but he hadn't been able to get any of us or any customers interested in it. Right when he and his family were leaving, I decided to buy it because he was only asking one dollar and I suddenly saw something that got me thinking about it. I saw two teenage boys walking up the street toward us. They were roughhousing and laughing and looked like they could use it. So I bought it and David was happy that he finally sold it before he left. The two teenagers thought the hammer was cool. They were playfully hitting each other on the head with it. They asked me how much it was. I could see that they really liked it, so I told them the price was four dollars. They thought it was a good deal, and they bought it. The parents all thought I was so clever and that was almost as good as the three-dollar profit I made.

I learned that you can look for opportunities in investing and act on one that makes sense. I definitely will stay on the lookout in the future for more investments that I can understand and follow through as well as my idea about the inflatable hammer.

Give your children as "normal" a childhood as possible. By this, I mean don't overindulge them with material treats, frequent trips, and other such goodies. This may take more discipline on your part than you want to employ, but if you care about parenting more than you do about self-indulgence, you'll apply yourself to the task.

Keep this firmly in mind in regard to discipline and self-indulgence: *Children need to earn their rewards.* It gives them something to look forward to, which is highly important in preparing for adulthood. Providing them with occasional carefully chosen treats is fine, but indulging their every whim is not only ill-advised but also not very smart. Indulging *your* every whim where your children are involved is even less smart.

Talk with your children about how they feel about their schoolmates being lavished with undeserved rewards. You can also talk with them about their feelings toward deserving schoolmates who do not receive rewards. Make each discussion an opportunity to educate them on what those rewards *are* and what they *are not.* Take the time to discuss the different kinds of happiness we all experience and the value of waiting, hoping for, and anticipating earned rewards. You will be helping them build awareness, which will serve them well throughout their lives. You will be enriching their appreciation of you as a thoughtful, caring parent by showing you care enough about them to bring them up well, so they won't become spoiled, self-indulgent adults, which would be to their detriment as well as yours.

Indeed, one of the greatest hazards of growing up in a wealthy family is the ease with which one can develop an attitude of entitlement. Constantly indulged with the latest toys, front-row seats at all performances, trendy trips, and an exemption from rules other children are expected to follow (such as being on time and not interrupting adults), many wealthy children grow up feeling they have an automatic *right* to the best and biggest share of everything life has to offer. Then, as their attitude of entitlement becomes increasingly ingrained, anxiety enters in as they begin to feel they *must* be on the top level of everything they experience, and otherwise something is wrong.

Stephanie became a client of mine when she was in her early twenties. A member of a prominent, wealthy family, she wanted help at first with relationships that weren't working. In actuality, she didn't have many friendships, and her relationships with family members were poor. During the first weeks of our work together, she seemed as interested in whether or not she could trust me as she was in the content of our sessions. Eventually, tentatively and subtly, she brought up her concern over an eating disorder.

I, of course, responded to her cue. Later, I found out, Stephanie had been aware that I had begun my career as an eating-disorders therapist. She was bulimic, she revealed, and was experiencing a lot of trouble with her problem. One of the most common traits of bulimics is perfectionism, and Stephanie's need to be perfect had resulted from growing up with a sense of entitlement. Predictably, as an adult on her own in a world that no longer pampered her with the privileges of her youth, she had turned her feelings of entitlement into extremely high expectations of herself, among them the obsession with having the "best" possible body.

Professional observations: *One of the main issues of bulimia is control. Stephanie had lost the illusion of control she had grown up with, so she created a focus on an area of her life over which she had a sense of complete self-determination. This was not a conscious effort, just her reaction to the uneasy feeling of standing on shifting sands as an adult. The first step in healing is awareness, so helping her acquire an understanding of her attitudes and behav-*

80

iors was a great start in her journey out of bulimia and into the freedom and autonomy of adulthood.

Instead of a sense of entitlement, we need to instill in our children the attitude that they are no better *and* no worse, no more *and* no less than anyone else. Years ago, I heard about a children's club of the backyard variety, created and run entirely by the children themselves, who had just three rules:

1. Don't act big.
2. Don't act small.
3. Be medium.

Wisdom from the mouths of babes? I think so.

Simple as it sounds, a far-reaching effort is demanded of parents if their children are to learn that privileges are meant to be enjoyed, honored, and perceived for what they are and what they aren't. If children are to learn that rewards are not bestowed habitually, they must also learn that rewards are *earned*, that they come, sometimes unexpectedly, as a treat for having *done* something. These lessons are critically important for children to learn because the attitude of entitlement is extremely hard to give up when they become adults, and there is nothing positive to be gained by those who stubbornly hang on to their presumption of privilege.

Betty, a well-dressed woman of fifty-eight with the unmistakable air of wealth, came into my office one day with deep concerns about her eldest daughter, Tricia. Thirty at the time, Tricia was extremely ambitious and deeply involved in the world of showing horses, Hunters in particular. Her mother had been motivated to finally seek help because of a highly disturbing incident she had witnessed at the last horse show she had attended.

Betty reported to me that Tricia did not have many friends and had never seemed interested in marrying. But she loved to ride. She also loved to win. At the show she'd attended, Betty saw that Tricia was doing well as a competitor, winning several classes. The incident that disturbed her so greatly, she then told me, occurred at the back gate of the arena where she was standing when Tricia walked out with her horse, carrying a second-place ribbon after an event in which she had just participated.

Before her daughter noticed her, Betty revealed, one of the other onlookers, a young girl, congratulated Tricia with unabashed admiration for the beauty and accomplishments of horse and rider. To Betty's consternation, Tricia strode past her effusive admirer, glaring straight ahead without acknowledging the congratulations. Deeply embarrassed, Betty understood instinctively why her daughter had behaved so rudely, for she had seen her react with anger when she fell short in any way. Betty knew that Tricia experienced second place as failure. Because of her family's wealth and social standing, Tricia felt she had to excel at everything she did, cutting herself no slack whatsoever when she failed to do so. Resolved to help her daughter with her destructive attitude, Betty came to see me soon afterwards.

Professional observations: Many inheritors feel both extreme pressure to be the best in everything they undertake as well as a sense of entitlement that this top territory belongs exclusively to them. These feelings are often exacerbated by extreme ambition and a sense of insecurity. Tricia had worked herself into a trap of emotions that were so intense she had grown inflexible in regard to her personal successes. Betty's only hope of reaching her daughter and helping her with her self-defeating demands on herself and her sense of entitle-

ment was to give her love, support, and acceptance. Tricia is not likely to change her attitudes and behaviors until she experiences enough pain that she is motivated to grow.

Instead of allowing children to become rooted in a debilitating sense of entitlement, cultivate in them the belief that their attitudes and choices will be the most important possessions they bring to whatever circumstances God places them in. Show them their challenge is to be happy and fulfilled in whatever worldly existence God chooses for them, including whatever material resources they are given, be they many or few. Help them to believe that, yes, they are meant to *shine* as they strive for excellence and that excellence can be achieved *whatever* their circumstances may be.

At the same time, teach them that the humble acceptance and appreciation of what God gives us is a paramount goal, that humility is a strength, not a weakness. This is another principle of happiness turned upside-down by the mainstream world. Let your children learn early that whenever they see arrogance and entitlement in their lives, they must find a way to replace it with humility and gratitude. Opportunities to inspire and strengthen our children by instilling in them these positive attitudes and behaviors start at a very young age.

Having learned this critical lesson, most people are sustained by it throughout their lives. Yet, sadly, some inheritors strive to insulate themselves from its liberating freedom—they struggle instead, to hang grimly on to their attitude of entitlement. The Tenth Commandment makes it clear why we must not do this: "You shall not covet your neighbor's house; you shall not covet your neighbor's wife ... or anything that belongs to your neighbor" (Exodus 20:17). Most certainly, we are not *entitled* to any of these things.

If you find your children fretting about others having more than they do, remind them of two things. First, many of those they envy probably envy others; perhaps they even envy *you*. Second, the Tenth Commandment teaches us to let go of envy, a wholly nonproductive and worthless emotion. Remember that God expects each of us to play the hand we've been dealt in life and to do so with a positive attitude.

Furthermore, in the midst of entitlement lurks an ironic twist. What can happen is that inheritors may unconsciously assume it is their birthright to satisfy their every desire, whatever it might be and whenever it may occur. In fact, they can suffer anxiety over how it would feel not to have every desire instantly met. Yet, ironically, for those accustomed to instant gratification in all things, the best scenario for their personal growth, and certainly for their spiritual growth, would be to have many of those wants go unmet.

Parents, therefore, can help their children's inner growth by allowing for failure, frustration, and striving in their young lives because these experiences lead to emotional maturity and a deepening sense of personal satisfaction. Overindulgence is all around us in our materialistic society, so much so that parents feel as if they're swimming upstream when they go against the current. But resist it they must because self-indulgence diminishes our potential and enslaves us, while self-control nurtures our potential and liberates us.

In his early forties, Matt is the inheritor of a substantial fortune that will be even greater after his father's death. Both of his parents were inheritors too. Despite the complicated and turbulent dynamics of his extended family, he enjoys a stable, rewarding relationship with his own family, due largely to the strong commitment he and his wife have made to their marriage. The appreciation and grati-

tude he has for his life has resulted from the personal struggles and triumphs he achieved by working through the early mistakes and pitfalls of his marriage, he says, as well as by coping with the financial shortcomings of his chosen career as director of a large theatrical organization.

His fervent desire is to pass along to his two sons and one daughter, all under the age of ten, the hard-earned sense of self-sufficiency and personal fulfillment that is now his after having taken so much for granted while growing up in a household of privilege and ease. "After all," he asks himself often, "why shouldn't they take everything for granted as I did? They really do have everything." If, therefore, he can do this important thing for his children, Matt feels, he will be preparing them for adult life, far better than he was prepared.

I've coached Matt in his noble mission, and he has followed through on every idea for encouraging gratitude that we have come up with together. His wife is highly supportive as well. He takes his children with him to work in soup kitchens. He chooses books for them to read and movies to see that depict how the rest of the world lives, particularly those less fortunate than they are. He sees to it that they always write thank-you notes and that they always express their gratitude, even for the smallest gifts or kindnesses they receive.

When they are given presents at Christmas or on their birthdays, he makes sure they always do as he has instructed: open one gift at a time with their total attention, and then get up and go to the person who gave it to them and look that person in the eye while saying thank you. When they say their prayers at night, he encourages them to include five things for which they are grateful. At the same time, Matt is gathering the courage to let them experience failure and deprivation instead of sheltering them, for how else, he reasons, will they be able to prepare themselves for those *inevitable moments when pain, disappointment, and misfortune will enter their lives?*

Matt and I both know there are many things he and his wife can do to nurture their children's sense of gratitude, appreciation, and humility. Still, his question (and mine) remains: Can parents actually instill these virtues in their children? Or can we only teach and encourage them to become the adults we hope and pray they will be? And what about our lofty goal of instilling compassion and character in the context of private schools, country clubs, expensive trips, box seats at performances, and other first-class privileges? Does instilling compassion and character in our children justify depriving them of the good things in life we are able to provide because of our wealth? As a result, will they look back on the deprivations and our "tough love" one day with bitterness or with gratitude?

In an ironic twist of perspective, made even more relevant by the horrific events of September 11, 2001, and their devastating aftermath, it is now evident that the generations of Americans who weathered the Great Depression and World War II emerged from these extremely trying times with a strength of character and lifelong attitudes of humility, appreciation, and gratitude that they otherwise might not have acquired. In their cases, they were self-taught by their own experiences, so the question lingers: Can children be taught gratitude, appreciation, and humility by their parents?

Professional observations: *Yes, I most certainly think they can be taught. Matt is doing it with conscious deliberation. Make no mistake about it, children learn by what they see their parents do. Matt's children will, indeed, benefit from his frequent examples, from the obvious manifestations of his regard for the qualities he is working to instill, not just by his words but by his deeds. For these fortunate children, the undeniable proof lies in their father's actions.*

At the same time, Matt is building character by allowing them to achieve on their own, thus acquiring a sense of competency. He is helping them by having them do whatever they can do for themselves. No doubt, private schools, country clubs, expensive trips, and other privileges of wealth can enhance the quality of children's lives, but only if the children are taught to accept these gifts with humility, gratitude, and appreciation, not with an arrogant sense of entitlement. To your dismay, however, you may not find many other inheritors who make humility, gratitude, and appreciation a priority in their children's lives. Matt is a rare, inspiring exception.

On a personal note, when I read Tom Brokaw's The Greatest Generation, *I kept thinking about the gratitude of the people described in his book. Most of them came from modest backgrounds. My own father certainly did. He worked extremely hard in his life to become hugely successful in business. He felt it a privilege, therefore, to provide me with educational opportunities, cultural enrichments, and financial security. Today, there is no doubt in my mind that he wanted only the best for me, that it was his fervent wish that I attain the finest life any parent could envision for his child.*

And yet, somehow overlooked, despite his best of intentions, was a certain insensitivity that my life of privilege and ease created in me. This happened despite my father's constant display of his own gratitude and appreciation for his own life. For instance, he loved getting dressed for work, he told me. To him, a business suit was a tangible symbol of his escape from the farm life of his youth, one filled with long hours and tedious, exhausting work. The worst part, he said, was that farmers can work so hard and do everything right, only to have inclement weather or other uncontrollable circumstances rob them of the accomplishments and rewards they have striven all year to achieve. The suit he put on each day was a literal

*reminder of the personal successes he won through determination
and hard work, successes no one could ever take away from him.*

*Throughout his life, my father remained grateful for his break-
through opportunity to be part of a successful business empire. To
him it was a giant step up from the hardscrabble farm life he had led
as a boy. It seems to me that now there are so few people who dress
up as a sign of true, heartfelt respect. That little gesture of respect is
something big I remember about my father. I know he didn't mean
to raise an ingrate, but somehow, in giving me so many of the things
he had lacked as a boy, this is what happened. It is something I have
worked my whole life to overcome.*

A friend of mine often uses this expression: "You never get enough
of what you don't want." Trying to get enough of what you think
you want can be an unconscious cover-up, you see, for what you
really want. Children, for instance, who are permitted to watch
too much television and thus want even more, or who are given
too many toys and want even more, become enslaved, resulting in
their potential for achievement being greatly reduced.

*Laura, a fourth grader, observed quietly as many of her classmates
were treated to family trips to Hawaii and other fancy resorts. She
was a girl fairly appreciative of her lot in life, yet she was starting to
feel she was missing out on something important. She felt her friends
were getting to do all these neat things while she wasn't, and it was
getting to her. "Why are we the only ones who don't go to Hawaii?"
she began asking her parents. "Couldn't we go there for spring vacation since everyone in my class already has?"*

*These remarks provided her parents with a precious opportu-
nity to empathize with her, to find out exactly in what way she felt
"left out" and "not grown up enough" and why these feelings made*

her sad. They were then able to explain exactly what had kept them from going to Hawaii (finances, inopportune timing because of obligations to younger siblings, and one parent's preference for other types of vacations). Finally, they encouraged her to contribute her ideas on how to make a trip to Hawaii possible sometime in the future.

Laura loved being asked to participate in this way. With her mom's research assistance she compared airfares and hotel prices, suggested alternate times of the year, and listed choices that would save them money. She offered to contribute part of her weekly allowance to a family kitty set up specifically for the trip. She talked to her younger brothers about their vacation preferences, a task for which she felt particularly well-suited since she had once been their ages herself and could empathize with them. She even inspired them to contribute part of their weekly allowances to the family "Hawaii vacation" kitty along with her.

Professional observations: Laura rose to the occasion and benefited from her parents' efforts to understand her feelings and include her in family planning. She had been presented with an opportunity to feel empowered and to work toward something that was highly important to her, and she reveled in her new leadership role and her new responsibility. Because of her personal investment in the Hawaii trip, I'm sure it will be a sweet reward for her.

As incongruous as it may sound, gratitude can develop from unfulfilled desires if we allow it to. I say this because heartfelt satisfaction and inner growth come from meeting life's challenges with courage and grace, from figuring out how to meet our adversities well, from weathering our disappointments and setbacks, and by acknowledging all the help we get along the way.

There are many levels of gratitude, of course, and parents can begin by introducing the most rudimentary of them to their children. They can start, for instance, by training them to write thank-you notes and explaining to them the importance of doing so. Parents can instruct their children on looking a friend in the eye and expressing their gratitude when a gift is received. Parents can teach children to return thanks for their food before eating a meal. Parents can exemplify and explain about tithing at church. There is so much we can do to instill in our children the importance and emotional rewards of gratitude, on whatever level, and it's never too early to start.

There is an episode of the old television series The Twilight Zone *in which a gangster dies and goes to his afterlife. There, he lives a life of complete luxury. He has beautiful women at his beck and call. He goes gambling and wins every time. He lives in opulent surroundings and consumes the finest foods and wines. Still, after a time he grows bored and frustrated because he never gets to* not *get what he wants.*

Eventually, he contacts the caretaker of his afterlife and tells him there must have been a mistake. He tells the caretaker he thinks he doesn't belong in heaven where all of his needs and desires are met. He tells the caretaker that this place is driving him nuts, that he wants to go to the other place. The caretaker tells him, "This is *the other place."*

There is also the element of *perspective* for inheritors to consider. Therefore, it is important for children of wealth to be exposed to how the "other half" lives. There are many ways to achieve this, such as helping out in a soup kitchen or participating in mission trips. Activities such as these go a long way in bringing personal meaning to the old saying, "I felt bad that I had no shoes, until I met a man who had no feet." There are also books that can intro-duce children to the world of those who have less of the world's riches than they do.

A woman I know has informed her children that once they graduate from college, the flow of money from their parents will end. Their mother and father have been happy to pay all their expenses through college, but the subsistence *will* end there, she and her husband have told them in no uncertain terms. In fact, it is still undecided in this family whether the children will inherit the wealth created by their father when he dies.

What the woman and her husband *do* agree on is that they want their children to experience how the rest of the world lives, how it feels to face the great questions, "How will I support myself? How will I handle life with only *me* to count on?" They encourage their children by telling them that the fear and insecurity they will surely feel when starting out on their own will probably be tempo-rary—for these are strong, capable children—and that it will be an experience and education they don't want their children to miss because it will hold them in good stead for the rest of their lives.

For many inheritors, however, their *inheritance* is the sole plan for the future. If such is the case, they should be taught instead to regard their inherited wealth as a *safety net.* One doesn't sit in the net and drift through life—or sit in the net and sink into the mire. The net is simply placed in the background of your life and used to relieve occasional anxieties. It is there while you work hard to achieve your greatest potential. I have heard many older inheritors express gratitude for the safety net they were pro-vided—and also for the fact that they were taught the conse-quences of its misuse.

The teaching of gratitude can be woven into children's every-day life. They can be taught to be good stewards of what they are given, starting at a very young age. Shopping together, for instance, presents many opportunities for such teaching. Here, I'm reminded of the fact that parents are always counseling through example, and this applies to shopping as well as to everything else children learn in life by observing and emulating us. It's up to parents, therefore, to be fully aware of the endless things they can teach through example, for they are imparting their *values* as well as their business and purchasing acumen.

Since it is a given that children will absorb most of their shopping skills from their parents, at the same time, these activities present priceless opportunities for us to pass along our values. For instance, how do you feel about paying for a pricey "name" brand when you can pay half as much for the same design and quality without the "name"? In other words, you can teach your child to choose shoes or apparel for reasons other than the fact that the brand name or label is "in" at the moment and the child wants to be instantly perceived as "with it."

Rather, teach your children to think for themselves instead of simply being followers. Instead of paying the price, whatever it happens to be, teach them to ask, "How much is it?" while asking themselves, "Is it worth the money? Would I be just as happy with something else less expensive?" rather than making the purchase simply because they can afford the price. Teach them that having the money is *not* an adequate reason to buy something.

This way, at an early age, they can be practicing their math as they question the values, adding and subtracting as they compare prices and the comparative worth of items. As they watch you pay for an item, you can reinforce their sense of gratitude by remarking, "Isn't it fortunate that we can just write a check or use a credit card to pay for this?" Of course, you need to explain that writing the check or using the credit card means that money is being spent!

Be straightforward, too, about your intentions regarding your children's inheritance. If you are providing them with a lifestyle full of privileges that meets all of their material needs, and you intend to bequeath your estate to charity instead of to them, *tell* your children of your altruistic aim. It would be both disrespectful and unkind not to inform them how you plan to send them out into the world—and *why*.

Nowhere is it written, of course, that you're required to pass along all of your wealth to your offspring. Indeed, if that is not your intention and you are now providing them with a luxurious and expensive lifestyle, then be certain you are preparing them adequately to go out on their own, and equip them with the educational, emotional, and spiritual resources they will surely need to make their way alone in a much harsher world than the one they have grown used to.

If, on the other hand, you fully intend to provide them inherited wealth, you still will need to equip them with the educational, emotional, and spiritual resources to live life well while coping with the allurements and distractions of financial ease. It is the same concern that all parents have, inheritance or no inheritance, in preparing their children for adulthood.

Be straightforward with them about how they need to be prepared to live in the real world, with an inheritance or without one. It would be unkind for you to bring them up on the best of everything and then surprise them by sending them out into the world to struggle on whatever income they can manage on their own. By the same token, I'm sad to say that some of the most extravagant losses of fortunes I have seen or heard of involve children who had no idea they were going to inherit wealth. Whether you plan to leave them an inheritance or not, you should inform them of what you plan to do.

Theo grew up in what he had perceived his whole life to be an upper-middle-class family living on a truly beautiful estate. His father, an inheritor, had died in a car accident when Theo was eight. Theo had an older brother, though the two had never been close, In fact, Theo had used the word weird *once in describing this brother who was only "loosely connected" to their large extended family.*

Theo's education and experiences, he told me, had not included the handling or understanding of money in any way. His mother had simply provided it whenever it was needed. Despite being a smart, creative freethinker, he had very little self-discipline and had drifted in and out of colleges for several years, never coming close to earning a degree. Finally, when he turned twenty-one, the family attorney, a lifelong acquaintance, asked the young man to come to his office, whereby he informed him of his inheritance— which Theo had known nothing about. And so, that afternoon he went on his way $1.8 million richer, a sum that took him barely nine years to spend entirely.

Professional observations: *Many inheritors receive their fortunes in this manner—as a bolt out of the blue. With this sort of scenario, the inheritance feels cold and strange; the receipt of the money is a shock. Inheritors cope in different ways, and some rise to the occasion of handling their unexpected good fortune well. But others, like Theo, find the subsequent journey a lonely one, which they often attempt to ease through spending. Preparing and educating children to receive an inheritance, therefore, is best begun when the inheritors are young. In this way, parents will ensure that the inheritor's legacy is a warm, enriching one rather than a cold, numbing shock.*

In addition, then, to the good examples set by parents, one of the best ways we can start teaching our children how to handle money is simply to give them an allowance. Certainly, too, the same wisdom inherent in providing an allowance or extra chores at home for the earning of additional money and proper counseling on spending, saving, and sharing this common form of "energy" applies equally to children in families with or without wealth.

The fact is, however, that whenever inherited wealth looms as a factor in a child's life, money-management issues almost surely will be heightened or exaggerated. If inheritors, therefore, are going to be good stewards of their wealth, proper money-management education is vital, and the sooner the better.

In his wise book, *Raising Resilient Children*, Dr. Robert Brooks points out that all children have three basic needs: first, the need to feel they belong and are connected; second, the need for self-determination and autonomy; and third, the need to feel competent. It is helpful to keep these basic needs in the forefront of your mind as you instruct them about money, and definitely later when you teach them about wealth.

Giving children an allowance directly addresses their need to belong, to feel connected. Because they receive this allowance simply for being members of the family, it is separate from their household responsibilities—chores such as putting dirty clothes in the hamper or making the bed or feeding the dog. These are the natural results of belonging to a family, and they reinforce the child's critical feeling of attachment. The consequences, therefore, of your children's neglect of household obligations should not be tied to their allowance. The allowance is simply unconditional.

The child's basic need for self-determination and autonomy can be addressed by providing choices on handling—spending, saving, giving away—their money as well as choices relating to household responsibilities. The simple skills of managing a budget or washing windows to earn money for a specific goal can provide youngsters with the same exhilarating sense of competence and accomplishment we all cherish as adults.

⌣⌐

Think about the difference between praise and encouragement. Praise is given for an outcome, an end achieved. Encouragement is given during the process of attainment. For instance, "Congratulations, son, that's great!" would be praise for an A on a child's math test. Encouragement would be, "Look at all the right answers on this matching test! See how your hard work is paying off!" Encouragement is the more effective of the two, and parents need to be on the lookout for opportunities to provide it as often as possible. By directing our comments to the process of attainment rather than its culmination, our encouragement is ongoing and continuous, thus making it more valuable than praise, which signifies an end. The constructive work of attainment is an important feeling for a child to get used to.

As for discipline, consider it a promise kept. In other words, if you promise an action or consequence, you *must* follow through on it. Many families have trouble making such promises, and many have trouble keeping them. Children need to know their parents' priorities and values and that there *will* be consequences for not living up to them. In short, they need to know what the family values are and what is *expected* of them. (It's best, therefore, if the children have some say in the making of those rules.) They need to know what the boundaries of their behavior are and what will happen if they overstep those boundaries. For instance: "If you steal a car, we *will* turn you in. We'll do everything we can to help you, but you have to face the consequences of your actions."

One family I know bases its boundaries on the Ten Commandments. As long as the children in this family live within the guidelines and values of God's Commandments, they are assured full parental support. In the true spirit of forgiveness, occasional youthful mistakes and transgressions are forgiven. This necessary discipline is imposed, after all, not for its own sake but to keenly impress on children the possible repercussions of repetitive, willfully destructive life choices. Therefore, the ultimate discipline of forfeiture of one's inheritance is imposed solely for such repetitive, self-destructive choices and only after the child has reached responsible adulthood, certainly never before the age of twenty-one.

This, then, is the foundation of character that parents can start building in their children very early on. But the effort must be thoughtful, diligent, and consistently sustained, for young people need the constant learning experiences involving family values and boundaries of behavior that are the building blocks of character. This is how their moral foundation is molded. The process starts early and remains constant and ever-present. In this manner, the child is best prepared for a solid, decent, and worthwhile life, particularly where inherited wealth is involved, for one day these questions will surely arise: "Is this child worthy of his inheritance?" "Can he be *trusted* with the family fortune?" "Is she capable of handling the challenges it imposes?" "Will he be willing and able to uphold the family standards when presented with its weighty stewardship?"

Audrey, thirty-eight, has been married for eight years and has two children, ages four and six. Her father, who has accumulated great wealth from several successful businesses that he founded, is used to

97

controlling the people and events in his business life and applies this commanding attitude to his family as well, she told me. Audrey is certain that he has set aside a large amount of his wealth in her name, but she has no idea how much. "He doesn't want me to know," she told me.

In her attempts to gain some control over her life, Audrey has asked the family's accountants and attorneys to educate her in regard to her financial assets and options, to little avail. "They're afraid of him," she said bluntly. "They only tell me what he wants them to tell me." There have even been times, she revealed, when they phoned him in her presence to ask if they could release the information she requested. Not wanting to demand their full cooperation or to go against her father in her desire to become financially responsible, Audrey has given up time and again, with growing frustration and resentment.

As an example, she tells of the house she and her husband recently built in the same city where they and her father both reside. "It's nice enough," she said, "but not the dream home I'd envisioned creating for myself and my family." What had prevented her from building her dream home was the usual confusion over exactly how much money she had to spend. As a result, Audrey felt guilty for not feeling grateful for the house she got because of her frustration over not getting exactly what she wanted. "It's not a matter of the money not being there," she said, "but that I don't have clear and free access to it."

Audrey's husband, whom she described as "a really nice guy who has a good job, works hard, and is easygoing about money," hasn't been of much help, she revealed. In fact, her relationship with her father has worsened since their marriage. "My husband is no support at all," she told me. "He says it's not his place to get involved." Meanwhile, her father continues to think Audrey is extravagant.

Audrey, on the other hand, despite not knowing the numbers involved, is convinced she is spending only a tiny fraction of the income already in her name. "I sneak around," she said, the resentment evident in her voice, "disguising my purchases from my father and hating myself and him for doing it."

Professional observations: *Many people would be surprised to hear how common Audrey's story is among inheritors. Dad doesn't realize the extreme frustration he is causing his daughter; instead, he himself feels frustrated at what he perceives as an utter lack of appreciation and regard for what he has given her. To him she seems totally out of control, unlike his employees, over whom he's able to exercise complete restraint. Theirs is a conflict of attitudes and behaviors resulting from a profound lack of communication. The two could start healing themselves by spending some proverbial time in each other's shoes.*

Sarah, a forty-five-year-old inheritor, had worked with me for months on resolving relationship issues with her husband. She had applied herself well and accomplished much, and we were nearing the end of our time together when she shared an insight with me. "It is a hard thing for me to talk about, because I've struggled with expressing it," she began. "My father created a great fortune and my parents gave me a life full of privilege, including a wonderful education. Even if there were some life lessons I lacked as I became an adult, I was given a lot by them."

Sarah is a writer, who for years had not been sure whether she wanted to be a journalist, novelist, biographer, or documentary writer. She had found jobs in all of these fields, and a few more before eventually settling down to write for a magazine—work she described as "suiting me well." It was my impression that her work was an important, positive part of her life. "My father died fifteen years ago," she went on, "leaving a small part of his fortune to me and to my siblings. Most of it he left to my mother.

"What he left me was enough so that I could live well and pursue my dreams, but not so much that I would be frivolous with the money or kick back and coast through life. As a result, I've had to be creative in finding ways to remain a full-time mom and have had to work hard at my profession. My husband has a good job, and we both contribute to the support of our lifestyle. There are times that I've felt financial pressure, but the truth is I have freedom, security, autonomy, and a sense of personal power over my life. Looking back, I think my father was brilliant and kind in leaving me the amount that he did."

Sarah backtracked for a moment. "What I meant when I said I struggled against talking about this is that because whenever I feel pressure financially, I find myself wishing he had left me more. This happens in spite of the fact that, because he didn't provide me with more financial ease, I've had to respond to my challenges with courage, creativity, and growing maturity.

"What I'm saying, I guess, is that I kind of like the struggle because I think it's good for me, and I know that my wise father knew it as well. Usually, the struggle pushes me in a spiritual direction, along the lines of 'When life gives you lemons, make lemonade.' Nor have my struggles to cope been debilitating. On the contrary, they have provided me chances to experience humility, to place my trust in God, and to stretch toward my fullest personal and professional potential."

Professional observations: *Wealth is relative. Even though Sarah has not yet inherited the majority of what will someday be hers, she* *is grateful for what she has received and recognizes the wisdom of her parents' choices. She already has made her life rich.*

As your children learn, therefore, to handle their allowance and the additional money they earn from working around the house (and later from neighborhood and summer jobs), you can begin acquainting them with the broader aspects and responsibilities of the financial stewardship that will one day be theirs. Again, the process is a building-block method of connecting practical experiences to moral values.

Provide each child with a ledger in which to record his or her income and expenditures. Encourage them to use it on an ongoing basis. Give them each a notebook and have them write in it all the ways they would like to spend their money. Periodically ask each of them to go through the list and assign a value to each of their choices ("1" through "10" or "A" through "F"). This will set the stage for a discussion of how *they* feel about their evaluations. Then go through the list with them yourself and assign a value to each of their choices (again, "1" through "10" or "A" through "F"). This time the stage will be set for a sensitive discussion of how they feel about *your* evaluation of *their* choices.

This would also be a good time to present them with alternate choices of higher moral value, without disparaging their own selections. You can repeat the evaluation process and dialogue at regular intervals to teach and reinforce your values. You might even hold family meetings with the intention of developing a family mission statement on using money well.

All members could be asked to contribute their thoughts on the subject, with everyone discussing the others' opinions. By giving your children a clear voice and the opportunity to participate in all matters of family planning (including financial management, philanthropy, and purchases that affect everyone), you are investing their places and roles in the family in a very real and loving way. All in all, these are excellent ways for parents to impart their moral values to their children in a cooperative, constructive environment, while instilling a sense of belonging.

At some point, around the age of eighteen or twenty-one, it may be a good idea to give your young inheritors some wealth to "try out." I hesitate to put a dollar figure on this recommendation, because in order for it to be significant, it should have some relationship to the amount of wealth that will be inherited. In order for this "trial" amount to seriously challenge the young adult, it should be far more than the inheritor has been responsible for before. For some families, therefore, $100,000 would be a significant amount; for some, the figure might be $250,000; for others, less or more. This is a highly individual figure.

The exact amount is a sensitive point, for it needs to be a sum of money that could be lost in that it comprises *training* for the young inheritor. Some families provide it outright; others require an intermediary in the form of a family member or advisor who will serve as a *financial personal trainer*, so to speak. The money may be given with or without restrictions, with or without attached stipulations and communicated hopes or wishes.

This brings us to important questions parents need to ask themselves, such as, "What are my own attitudes toward family wealth?" "Is it more important for me to preserve my wealth or to use it to empower my children and facilitate the autonomy that will be vital to their spiritual fulfillment?" Asking such questions of yourself—and *answering* them—is critical to your children's happiness, for they will learn best from your examples. The most important values in life are *caught*, not taught. They will be *lived out by you* in front of your children.

CHAPTER SIX

The Vital Component of Education

MOST OF US REGARD EDUCATION as a primary means to the important end of making a living. In fact, this is probably the reason that most Americans would give for valuing their education.

Many inheritors, however, feel no sense of urgency or need in this regard. To them an education may seem optional. This is a mistake, for while there are people who do well enough without one, they are exceptions to the rule that a good education is critical to everyone's future, regardless of financial considerations.

Yet some inheritors find themselves thinking, "Why bother?" I answer that there are many good reasons to "bother" and very few reasons, if any, *not* to bother. In fact, I can't think of a single one. First of all, in the same sense that physical exercise keeps our bodies strong and healthy, an education keeps our minds agile and active. Call it the "use it or lose it" reason for earning a degree. Pursuing an education is also a great means of instilling self-discipline, and the wonderful thing about self-discipline is that it can be applied to everything in our lives—again, regardless of financial considerations.

Other benefits of a solid education are a trained mind and the ability to track and develop elaborate thought processes, imaginative concepts, and genuine creativity. There is also the immeasurable enrichment that comes from a continual exposure to new ideas and information. All in all, the mental rewards and emotional empowerment of a sound education should not be under-estimated by inheritors or anyone else.

Nor does it actually matter what higher degree you earn, only that you *acquire* a degree, not just for the degree itself but for all the attendant benefits of its diligent pursuit. You'll never regret earning a degree from an accredited institution of higher educa-tion, for having it tells the world and, more importantly, reminds *you* for the rest of your life that you do, indeed, possess the intel-ligence, tenacity, and grit to pursue whatever achievement you aspire to and to follow through on your goals.

Hearkening back to self-discipline (by which I mean self-control and the sense of empowerment that comes with the ability to make good choices), I can't stress enough that it is one of the most important strengths you can develop and pass along to your children. What a gift to a child! Some fortunate youngsters are born with a natural ease in developing self-discipline, while others seem to need considerable help, but all children can benefit from their parents in attaining this invaluable trait. Certainly all our efforts on their behalf are worthwhile, for self-discipline at an early age is a proven indicator of success as an adult.

Nor can the process of instilling self-discipline begin too soon. Children must regard school, at whatever age, as their "work" as well as their enjoyment. They need for their parents to respect their class schedules—and not keep them out of school for frivolous reasons or extra vacations. Yet this basic require-ment often calls for more dedication than some wealthy parents can muster.

Think for a moment, though, what message you are sending your children, what priorities you are instilling in them, when you blithely release them from their school commitments to take them off to play. Are you telling them, in effect, that their schoolwork is optional and less important, in fact, than their immediate gratification—and yours? How will they come to respect and value their "work" if *you* plainly don't? Remind yourself that there will be plenty of school vacations to savor with your children, but the precious opportunities to help them achieve self-discipline must not be squandered, whatever your forfeited pleasures.

There's something else that frightens and intimidates some inheritors about securing an education. The exact nature of the fear varies from person to person, but most often it masquerades as laziness. Those who have fallen into this negative mind-set need to seek help in extricating themselves from its enervating grasp in order to examine and identify exactly what it is that scares them. For some it may be self-doubt, for others a fear of failure, or the inability to measure up to expectations, or perhaps an unwillingness to sustain the requisite effort and commitment. Whatever their fear of achievement might be, they need to summon the courage to maximize their potential and achieve their full measure of self-development. Education is an essential step in this journey.

There is one caution to consider, however. Remember that a college degree and possibly a graduate degree are simply tools toward the achievement of a higher end. Even though the pursuit of a college education is enriching, worthwhile, and fulfilling, do not get stuck in it for its own sake. It is a means to an end, a journey with a destination.

Over the years, I have met several inheritors who have become perpetual students, retreating deeper and deeper into academia, not as a means toward an end but as an end in itself. And though other factors have been involved, a common denominator I have observed in them is a comforting familiarity with a diverting lifestyle that has made the necessary leap into the "real" world unsettling and scary. Like Peter Pan who never wanted to grow up, perpetual students unwilling to take responsibility for their lives and a productive future will not find true fulfillment.

An education, therefore, can be another incentive in the reinforcement of proper values in our children. Parents can set up a college fund as part of a trust incentive whereby the child receives a monetary "reward" when a bachelor's or master's degree or other professional degree is achieved. Thus, the financial gift is the "effect" and the earned degree is the "cause" of the parents' values-guided benevolence.

It is important to stress that a college fund of this sort needs to be set up so it will not be misused. The creator of such a trust probably will want to ensure the inheritor's timely transition from school to career. This can be achieved through an additional "reward" in the form of a financial gift for graduating in an agreed-upon number of years. Most estate-planning attorneys are aware of the sensitivity and care with which these incentive trusts must be designed, for the consequences can be exemplary or unfortunate. At best, they can impart values to the heirs and empower them. At worst, they can make inheritors feel controlled and trapped in childish behaviors, sometimes even challenging the values of other family members involved.

Nancy, who is sixty-seven, came to me with her growing frustration over her forty-two-year-old son. He was making a career, she said, of collecting academic careers and $100,000 with each degree he earned, as provided in a trust created by her deceased father. There had been no limit placed on the number of degrees he could earn, and her son "loved being a student," she related.

There are worse fates than being a perpetual student, Nancy explained. Nonetheless, she felt her son was misusing his grandfather's gift. So far, she revealed, she had been unable to persuade him to take on any other lifestyle. Reasoning with him was her only recourse in that she had no legal power to alter the trust. I helped her in accepting those choices of his over which she had no control. Interestingly, after she had worked hard to understand her son's lifestyle and not make it a bone of contention between them, he embarked on a research career in one of his many academic disciplines.

Professional observations: *While it is admirable for parents to thoughtfully teach their values to their children, including using monetary rewards to do so, the way the tools (such as an incentive trust) are set up needs to be very well thought out. In setting up an incentive trust similar to the one in this story, be sure you are working with an estate-planning attorney who is experienced and willing to think through any possible weaknesses in your plan.*

Lauren, on the other hand, attended one of my workshops in search of anything that might help her as a board member of her family foundation. From a very large extended family, at the age of twenty-seven she was already an impressive young woman. Many years before, her grandfather had set up an incentive trust, building into it the opportunity for sound discretion and wise choices.

Upon her graduation from an MBA program, Lauren had earned the right to secure a large sum of money from the trust for the purpose of starting a business. She had her heart set on establishing an interior-design firm and, in fact, before beginning her postgraduate studies had secured the necessary design education and training she needed for the livelihood of her choice.

Subsequently, she presented a business plan—a requirement of the trust—to the trustees, all of whom were members of her extended *family, and received $250,000 to launch her venture. When I became acquainted with her, Lauren's business was going well, and the gracious sense of stewardship and responsibility she held for the younger members of her family was evident in all of her questions and comments at the workshop.*

Professional observations: *Lauren was part of a large family for whom incentive trusts had been working well for decades. It is truly inspiring to meet such responsible inheritors. They are typically happy, confident, competent, generous, and exude a sense of purpose. It is important to note, too, that in her family there was a culture of cooperation with the values and character-building facilitated by the trusts. Nurturing that culture was one of the main functions of the older family members.*

With or without a formal education, inheritors often reach adulthood with an unrealistically benign view of the world. This can be the result of delayed emotional development and is definitely a consequence of the padding and cushioning that wealth often provides against life's harshness and perils. Hence, these two characteristics—delayed emotional development and an unawareness of life's dangers—are common to many inheritors.

When young adults who have already inherited a fortune are in their late teens or early twenties, they are particularly susceptible to boredom and outside influencers. Most people understand what boredom is, and when an inheritor has all the energy of youth and is in the natural time of life for character-building, receiving a fortune can be confusing. We live in a society in which the acquisition of money and the establishment of financial strength is a large and common reason for constructing a work life. If that motivator is taken away from a young adult, then the natural business of getting started as an adult by learning to take care of oneself can be compromised. (It should be noted here that giving young inheritors a small percentage of their eventual wealth while they are still young can be educational and beneficial.) Often the young inheritor just doesn't have the maturity or the necessary life skills to handle an entire fortune well.

The Smith brothers, Tim and Andy, were in their early twenties when their father died instantly in a terrible car accident. Each inherited $15 million. Their mother was not involved in the accident. She was still living and received an inheritance as well. The boys' fortunes were in trusts, but the terms of the trusts were so lenient that basically they could have money whenever they wanted it. The family lifestyle had always been large and had always included thrills. Now the boys had plenty of money, and they lost any sense of direction they might have developed.

For them, life became defined by the next "thrill." Would it be speed, as in skiing, boats, or cars? Would it be racing? Or women, maybe five instead of one? Or maybe drugs? There's certainly no lack of places to look for thrills. And when you're young, fun-loving, and have millions of dollars to spend, it isn't hard to attract "outside influencers," people hanging on and sapping the money from you.

This is what happened to Tim and Andy. Many "investments" and businesses were offered to each of them. Neither of these young men had acquired business savvy, and their business experience became one bad deal after another. There are many salesmen and agents (outside influencers) who can make all kinds of ideas sound lucrative and appealing to whatever weaknesses a potential buyer may have. Once in a while, Tim or Andy would make a little money, but mostly the trend was a downward spiral.

Tim, the older brother, married, settled down in his hometown of Seattle, and never really worked. He invested and managed his wealth, but he didn't do it well. There was another factor—pride—that entered in, too. And so, as the years marched on and as his wealth dwindled, Tim didn't want people to know about his declining fortune. Sometimes he felt pressured into making investments based strictly on his pride. Because he was a likable person, a lot of people were sorry that things went the way they did for him, but within fifteen years, the money was entirely gone. Eventually, even though he had set up small trusts for his three children, he had to deal with their disappointment and disillusionment over not inheriting the wealth he had always promised them. What's more, the children's trusts had been set up as leniently as his own, and their inheritances were also quickly spent.

Andy, Tim's younger brother, tried marriage in an attempt to settle down, but his lifestyle was just too wild. Charming, funny, and personable, as eager as his brother to chase the next high, the next thrill, he succumbed to drugs, women, and car racing. He also flew planes. He moved to Florida and was living life in the fast track, which can resemble a life of leisure but is far more destructive. The drugs became a bigger and bigger part of his life. He began dealing and used his planes to run the drugs. It became his life for several years, but after some bad deals and the huge spending required to support his flamboyant lifestyle, Andy's inheritance was gone as well.

When their mother died, it was found that she, too, had spent most of her inheritance, for she had lived large as well and had also trusted some not-so-honorable outside influencers. So these two brothers, now in their fifties, have had a rough ride. Both of them came into young adulthood with a fair share of strengths, but neither of them found ways to use those strengths to build lives for themselves.

Professional observations: *The tragedy in this story is that for each of these brothers, the person he could have become was lost. The mix of youth, wealth, aimlessness, and no guidance proved to be an explo-*

sive cocktail. If these boys had been educated financially as they were growing up and provided with guidelines, even in the trust documents (possibly a "cause and effect" or incentive trust), they may have had a better shot at fulfilling their lives instead of dissipating them.

A common reason inheritors develop late emotionally is that no one walks willingly into the kinds of experiences that tend to mature us, and many inheritors are quite successful in avoiding maturing experiences altogether. Education, unfortunately, is not in and by itself a character-building event when approached with vague intentions, but it still can provide some stepping stones for internal resiliency and expansion. For instance, simply hanging in there when the going gets tough can be a hugely worthwhile endeavor. Yet many inheritors with little at stake in forfeiting their education miss out on wonderful opportunities for emotional development and growth.

A common reason inheritors develop late emotionally is that no one walks willingly into the kinds of experiences that tend to mature us, and many inheritors are quite successful in avoiding maturing experiences altogether.

Dan came to me for help in completing his master's degree. At the age of thirty-five, he had a twelve-year history of educating himself on the graduate level, but most of his classes resulted in "Incompletes." His wife had become thoroughly disgusted with his educational "career," as she called it, and was no longer supportive of his efforts in the least.

In truth, Dan longed to be out in the professional world doing the work he dreamed of, in a field that was his passion, but this career demanded the educational credentials he was striving to achieve. However, there seemed to be many stumbling blocks in his path, mostly of his own creation. For one thing, he had a lot of trouble following through on the work necessary to complete his classes. For another, the standards he set for himself in the classroom were unrealistically high.

One of the immediate goals we worked on together was his completion of the papers and projects assigned to him in class, regardless of the mediocrity he felt he was producing. In order to accomplish this, he came to realize that he had to relinquish his dream of only turning in work that was stellar and worthy of publication. In other words, he had to quit setting impossibly high goals and concentrate on the mundane but necessary task of earning satisfactory grades in order to pass his courses.

Extremely intelligent, articulate, and clearly capable of achieving the career to which he aspired, Dan felt handicapped by living his life in the huge shadow of an immensely successful grandfather. It had been painful for him, therefore, to complete assignments that were merely passable, knowing he could do much better and always judging his efforts through the critical eyes of his grandfather. Still, he was making progress, for in the past his self-imposed, too-high standards had kept him from turning in the work at all.

Another factor contributing to his chronic scholastic failures—one common to inheritors—was that there were no financial consequences attached to his sabotaging one school term after another. Dan's inheritance was large enough that such wasted expenses posed no importance to him whatsoever. And so we kept working on his long-held fears of lowering the performance bar for his class projects from the idealistic to the necessary, and eventually he was able to graduate. Now he holds a job, which is a solid step on his way to the career of his dreams, and he feels a great sense of accomplishment.

***Professional observations:** It can be easy to indulge in defeating yourself with perfectionistic tendencies when there are no financial* *consequences to clinging to unrealistically high standards that cannot be met. Until a person takes a conscious look at how perfectionism is at work in his or her life, it will create constant disappointments and feelings of defeat. For a variety of reasons it is easy to become perfectionistic while growing up surrounded by excellence. Add to this the lack of motivation that can result from zero financial need, and the equation can be a high-octane formula for stalling out.*

One useful question that can arise in the course of securing an education is "Why me?" This question can surface anywhere or anytime, of course, in or out of an academic setting. It is one that students often pose to themselves when faced with the challenge of getting on with their adult lives. In the expansive, inner-directed environment of learning and coursework, inheritors can find themselves reflecting on their good fortune and eventually asking the question "Why me?"

"Why *me*?" they ponder, often guiltily, "Why do I have all this wealth that I can spend freely on anything and everything I want while others have to struggle just to pay their rent?" Such thoughts pose a significant early step in the awakening of the sensibilities of an inheritor. And the answer, of course, is extremely significant. Yes, indeed, why *you*?

"Why *me*? Why do I have all this wealth that I can spend freely on anything and everything I want while others have to struggle just to pay their rent?"

As your education trains you to think clearly, while the rest of your personal growth imbues you with vital spiritual principles and enhances your emotional skills, you will be able to work out the answer to this question for yourself. And answer it you must, not merely sweep it under the rug. I can't stress enough the importance of gathering the courage to answer this question of "Why me?" to your

Yes, indeed, why *you*?

complete satisfaction, for it is critical to your future sense of purpose and happiness.

⌒

Having pointed out the merits of a traditional education, I also acknowledge that each of us has to take our own path through life. And our education continues, of course, in all kinds of non-traditional venues for learning, including the highly touted University of Life and the painful School of Hard Knocks. Ultimately, all of us put ourselves in situations that force us to learn what we need to know. Sometimes these choices are intentional—deliberate moves on a definite career path. More often, our lifelong learning evolves from personal curiosity or a developing interest, the result of tentative efforts at finding our true riches in life.

Adventure travel, for example, can be packed with eye-opening and emotionally enriching experiences. No price tag can—or should—be put on a lifelong, open-ended education in the ways of the world, as long as it stretches you but doesn't break you. Occasionally inheritors, hungry to find out what life is "really" about, journey to faraway cities and countries, sometimes even changing their names to become anonymous and free to find their own happiness and self-fulfillment.

Kimberly first came to my office when she was in her late twenties. She had chosen Portland for her exploration of life because Oregon's natural resources suited her love for the great outdoors and because of Portland's widespread reputation as a friendly city. As a member of a prominent Eastern family with a last name recognizable anywhere in the country, Kimberly had changed her last name to gain the anonymity she felt was her first requirement for experiencing life as a "normal" person.

Her family, she revealed, was not supportive of her self-styled education, but enough unconditional love existed between them that she was able to keep in touch and not sever her ties completely. As awkward as the tenuous connection felt at times, it was keenly important to Kimberly. In fact, she had come to see me because she was uncomfortable with the deceit of her name change and its tacit disavowal of her family and heritage. In order to get a job, pay taxes, and secure credit, she had been forced to change her name legally, and she used it with her friends, of course.

What she hadn't anticipated was the distance she had to introduce into her personal relationships because of her secret. Together, we worked on ways she could foster a feeling of closeness with friends despite her necessary "deceit." Eventually, though, she came to realize she could not sustain any real relationships within the guise of an anonymous self. Kimberly had learned about trying to build trust where honesty is withheld. It is a painful but valuable lesson she will always remember.

Professional observations: *Discovering the detrimental effect that secrets can have on personal relationships was not among the lessons Kimberly thought she would learn. But the key point of any education is that it holds many surprises, some uplifting, others painful, and often both, as in Kimberly's case. She also learned the frustration and humiliation of working for a difficult boss without the context of an influential family name to buffer and protect her. With that frustration and humiliation, however, came strength, self-discovery, and humility as well. Her education, therefore, was valuable to Kimberly even though it came without a degree.*

For inheritors, there are many nontraditional education choices such as internships and apprenticeships, travel and residency in foreign lands, mission and charity work, mentoring (both as a mentor and one being mentored), and many others, I'm sure, beyond my awareness. Don't underestimate the importance of this learning to your emotional and spiritual growth. Regardless of what form your schooling takes, it should be an ongoing, vital part of your life.

An inherent quality of education is that it broadens the student. If you don't get educated, you run the risk of living your life with tunnel vision. There's a danger in thinking that things *have* to be a certain way in your life because that is how they have always been. You grow up in the finest neighborhood in town, a member of exclusive clubs, attending the best private schools, enjoying front-row seats to every performance you attend, and you become an adult thinking things *have* to be that way, accepting that they *will* be for the rest of your life.

The shock comes when you find out that they *won't*, when you're suddenly, somehow anonymous, on an equal basis with the public you once felt so far above. It's a hard, almost overwhelming adjustment, one you're not sure you can make and certainly feel you don't deserve. You want—no, you *need* for things to be the way they've always been, but now there's the fear that the resources required for keeping them that way are gone. No doubt it's scary, but it can also be thrilling to leave a world of security and privilege to enter a life of anonymity and challenge, where everything you receive is *earned* by you, not simply placed in your lap. Or there's the shock that comes when you find out how much of life you have to give up to stay so far above real life experiences.

There are two sides, you see, to a life of privilege. I have had several young clients who, like Kimberly, came to Portland from places where their families are well-known, for the explicit purpose of experiencing a life of anonymity, where everything they have they must earn themselves. It takes courage to do this. For some inheritors, such a bold transition becomes a permanent, necessary part of the way things must be for them from now on. For others, it is a simple experiment, a way to build courage, confidence, humility, spirituality, and the inner resources necessary to making their lives their own.

It is not uncommon for a young inheritor to develop an intense desire to find out what life would be like without recognition as a "rich person." Sometimes this desire for anonymity is coupled with a need to acquire a personal competency or the experience of making it on one's own. The ways in which people go about achieving this independence or autonomy vary tremendously. For instance, an inheritor from a high-profile, well-known family almost always must move to another city to acquire a measure of anonymity. Teri was thirty when she came to see me in the wake of just such a life-altering experience.

An accomplished equestrian who had fallen in love with horses at any early age, her parents had given her riding lessons and even had bought her a horse when she was in the eighth grade. Teri had treasured every moment she spent riding and was thrilled when she was allowed to trade up for a better horse in high school. Devoting as much of her time to her passion as her parents would allow, she was voted president of the Junior Hunt Club during her senior year. Although all she wanted to do was ride, her parents insisted she go on to college. Her choice of a college, of course, was one with an excellent equestrian program.

At this point in her life, Teri was not a particularly grateful child, and the compromise set up an attitude of deprivation in her. The academic part of the deal was merely a nuisance, something she put up with but resented because she felt she could not optimally develop her riding skills without devoting her full-time attention to the cherished endeavor. Teri made it through college but never lost her feeling of deprivation and anxiety over needing to ride more. Upon attaining her degree, she immediately went to England to live out her dream of excelling in her beloved sport. Enrolling in a prestigious riding school, she worked hard at honing her equestrian skills. But there's an ironic twist to the story.

In the spring of her senior year in college, as she was completing her major in art history, Teri had taken a course that literally shook her awake intellectually. It awoke in her the odd feeling, on the eve of her graduation, that during the past four years she had missed out on some of the most important opportunities of her life by remaining fixated on her sport at the expense of everything else. Upon completing her riding program in England, she returned home and went back to school to earn a master's degree in art history.

When we met, she related some recent experiences that were significant and which she felt had provided some perspective on her fitful journey through education and riding. She had come to understand that she had been angry, even sullen as a result of her perceived deprivation, resulting in her own loss, she realized. What could she do now to heal the harmful attitudes she had developed over a decade ago, she wanted to know? She had learned a lot in the five years since earning her master's degree, she said sadly.

Teri had ridden a little during her years in graduate school, she revealed, but this time the emphasis had been on her studies, instead of vice versa. When she completed her graduate work, however, she decided to ramp up her involvement with riding once again. She bought some property and developed it into a horse farm; the venture proved financially successful for two reasons. First, real-estate values had increased at a healthy pace during the three years that she owned the farm. Second, her father kept a close watch over the business enterprise and her expenditures.

In this interim of her life, Teri trained and showed horses, which had been her lifelong ambition, but she found to her surprise that she was lonely at this beautiful farm in a remote, pastoral setting. She was single, doing exactly what she wanted, or so she had thought, and yet felt a growing awareness of her longing for close relationships with people, not just her horses. Without being aware of the process, she had isolated herself, she realized.

Soon afterwards, already thinking about selling the farm, she was asked by Jay, an accomplished, well-known trainer from the East Coast, to ride for him on a buying trip up and down the West Coast. Feeling complimented at being chosen for the position, she promptly agreed, and after a week of test-riding all sorts of young jumpers, some barely broken, the trainer, evidently impressed, asked her to accept a permanent position on his farm in New York. Again, she immediately said yes, put her farm up for sale, chose two of her favorite horses, and drove with them to New York, thrilled at the opportunity to be known and recognized solely for her riding skills and to be closely involved with people who shared her passion for horses, but also pleased at the prospect of living across the country where her family wasn't known.

At first, Teri related, it was exciting to meet and associate with other riders, to interact with the veterinarian staff, the various owners, grooms, and managers, and to be living, working, and riding in a completely new setting. After only a few weeks, however, something happened to change her newfound sense of being at the right place at last. The trainer informed Teri that one of her horses was "no good," was not reliable as a show horse and never would be, and therefore should be removed from his stable. She met this unsettling information with a great deal of resistance. She knew the horse had some minor problems, Teri told the trainer, but she had won many championships on him and regarded him as the best horse she had ever owned.

Her arguments fell on deaf ears, however. Jay was adamant about getting rid of the horse and was skilled enough to amplify his reasons for wanting to do so. Eventually, with a heavy heart, Teri complied. She donated the horse to a nearby school with a riding program. She did it, she told me, because she was afraid that if she insisted on keeping the horse, she either would lose her position or be ostracized. That wasn't the end of the matter, however. A few weeks after her beloved horse's sad departure, the trainer told Teri that the second horse she had brought was too small a mount for her and that he would sell him for her as a children's horse. Again she met this proposal with resistance, but again he won.

Teri had paid $20,000 for the horse as an unbroken two-year-old and had trained him herself. Though admittedly small, he had proven to be talented, an easy ride, and a fun jumper. Nonetheless, the trainer informed her that since he did not like small horses, he didn't want him around. Soon after, Teri entered her second beloved horse in a show where the trainer sold him, later presenting her with a check for $2,500.

"At that point in my life," Teri told me, "I didn't understand money very well. It should have been perfectly obvious to me that this didn't add up, and I should have insisted on a lot more information. But I felt intimidated. The money I had used to buy the two horses was given to me by my father. It made me sick to lose so much of my investment, but I felt I had no real control over the events leading up to it. I would have done just about anything to ensure that I could continue to work and ride at the stable. There were some interesting and extraordinarily talented horses for me to work with, I reasoned, and Jay was an extremely accomplished teacher. A multi-

faceted individual, he didn't ride much professionally anymore but diligently coached all of the training."

Along with her developing skills under his expert tutelage, however, Teri experienced a number of unsettling incidents, one of which she related to me: "One of the high points for me was working with him alone with just one horse. Most of his horses were exceptionally talented green horses. All jumpers. Really, I had never felt springs like that and the level of talent in general in those horses was an entire league above anything I had ever experienced on the regular U.S. show circuit. We used to warm them up over four- and four-and-a-half-foot fences.

"I remember one day when he and I were working alone, he had me schooling a big, agile horse over five-foot one-stride and no-stride in and outs. They were set up in a grid pattern and there were a lot of them. When I was in the air over one, he would say, 'OK, right' or 'OK, left,' indicating which way I was supposed to turn next. It was intense since up until then I'd never had to be that quick about maneuvering right and left. It was the first time. We did the exercise a lot after that, but I'll always remember that first time, because at the end of it—and I thought I'd done pretty well—he said, 'I'm going to teach you to ride if it kills me.'

"Frankly, I was shocked at how unimpressed he was with my skills. But on the other hand, I appreciated the commitment I heard in his voice. I was grateful for all the challenges he had given me, but I felt kind of adrift. This was an outgrowth of the estrangement that had begun with his insistence I part with both of my horses. I didn't even have any money to show for it. They were just losses, and I keenly felt the resentment over it."

Shortly after that incident, Teri continued, he began trying to sell certain horses to her despite the fact that she didn't have that kind of money, and she told the trainer so. Embarrassed to tell her father about disposing of her horses, she knew that asking him for help was out of the question. She felt increasingly foolish, but her desire to preserve her job and lifestyle remained overwhelming. The break in her emotional logjam finally came one evening. Driving home from work, she passed a local bar and noticed a truck that belonged to Dennis, one of the grooms at the stable. He was a quiet and genuine person, and he had always been kind to her.

Teri decided to stop at the tavern and see her friend. "As we sat there talking," she said, "he must have decided I needed some help. 'I know you want to ride,' Dennis told me, 'and you're a good rider, but you're out of your league here. Go home. If you stay, you'll be eaten alive.'" Though startled to be told the truth so bluntly, Teri instinctively knew Dennis was right, but she also felt deeply disappointed over so much loss of herself that had resulted from her quest for excellence and self-fulfillment. She realized she had been naïve, thoroughly lacking in the worldliness she needed to handle herself better. She also doubted she would ever attain the anonymity she craved, because she realized something else even more disconcerting.

This trainer in whom she had invested her hopes and dreams had met her, after all, through another trainer in her hometown, where her wealthy family was well-known. As she thought back over the events during those months in his employ, she became certain she had been targeted by him as a lucrative source of income. This realization made her feel even more foolish for having thought she could ever attain a reputation and career solely as a top rider. In addition, the sense of competence and achievement she had worked so hard to acquire was even more disappointing because she had completely lost her bearings, she felt. And so she came home to heal.

Professional observations: *When I met Teri after her return, we began the tough work of searching for lessons in her experiences to* help define and develop her strengths. She began by forgiving herself for her naïve choices at the defining crossroads she had encountered in New York. She had been correct in her instincts that acquiring competency as a rider would be an important strength for her, she affirmed. She was able to acknowledge that she had, indeed, attained competency and mastery as an equestrian and that in many ways it had provided her with stepping stones to the future.

By refusing to buy the horses from the trainer to protect her job, she had also put the brakes on her emotional and financial losses. They would have been much greater if she had acceded to his further manipulations. She also discovered from the defining events of New York that the horse world was not where she wanted to spend her life. What she really wanted, she realized, was a good marriage and a happy family. And she realized too that this life would not mix well with the lifestyle she had pursued so avidly in the world of horses and the idealized circumstances which she had ultimately found to be illusionary.

She was beginning, finally, to move out of the dark side of wealth.

The Need to Work

GET A JOB. PAID OR UNPAID. It doesn't matter which, but it must be a real job in which you feel productive. Create the work for yourself. Or do it for someone else. Whether you work for free or for pay doesn't really matter, but you *need* to work. People who don't work become shallow, bored, boring wastelands.

There are many fulfilling jobs, and you have the privilege of finding yours. If you don't need to earn income, don't be distracted or misled by the salary issue. For example, if you're a woman and you have a child, you have the greatest work on earth: being a mom. And if you're in a financial position to make a success of this emotionally rewarding career, don't hire a nanny. Don't use daycare. Do it yourself. What could possibly be more productive than bringing up a child well? Nothing!

Of course, no one gets paid for this kind of work. Then again, there are many great jobs for which there is no pay. Volunteer positions can be challenging and just as validating as paid employment. In fact, pro bono work may even offer some advantages. For one thing, volunteer jobs are usually part-time. Also, you might easily be able to create the exact volunteer position you want, something much harder to achieve when pay is involved. But whether the job is salaried or not, just don't fool yourself into thinking you don't need to work. Everyone needs to work, whether or not they need the money. One of the biggest consequences of not working is that your spiritual life will suffer. Vacations and sabbaticals are great, but it's important to have something to take a vacation from—and work to come back to.

If you decide on paid work, you will probably find that you feel differently about your earned income and your passive income. By the latter I mean income that is typically earned by investments and which rolls into your life on a regular basis regardless of any effort or lack of effort on your part. Many inheritors have passive income from their inherited wealth.

Most inheritors who do paid work experience these two kinds of income differently. On one level, of course, it's all money, and to any outsider both forms of income might appear the same. For inheritors, however, the income from their inherited wealth may pose some symbolism and/or have unwritten rules associated with it. At the same time, they may perceive different symbolism and/or purpose associated with earned wealth.

Another work-related challenge is the tendency to quit when the going gets tough. As in love relationships, you will need to come up with your own unique motivation to stick out the tough times, since you won't be motivated by your salary as are most non-inheritors.

In my own life, my father taught me only a few things about money. One of them was this: "You will receive a great deal of money from me. Always keep it in your name. Don't let some boy take it from you." I had a lot of trouble with marriage in those early years, and I'm sure that from my father's point of view, all my relationships looked unpredictable to him, for he was quite clear about this advice. Consequently, I have kept what he gave me in my name. Though he died many years ago, his advice remains an unwritten rule in my life. Aside from the wisdom I see in it, I keep it out of love and respect for him.

Over the years, as I have been blessed with the ability to stay in a very good marriage, I have sometimes felt separate from my husband financially because of this particular attitude of mine. So, after we had been married for several years, I came up with a plan. I opened a joint investment account with both my husband's and my name on it. Into this account, I put all of the profit from the money I earn in my work. I only put money into it; I don't take any out. I find that I get a great feeling of building something financially for *us*. Symbolically, this is a big deal for me. Probably also relevant to my good feeling about this plan is that while my husband understands and appreciates how meaningful this is for me, it's really a minor blip on his emotional landscape. He's a secure guy.

Will had worked for almost twenty years in the high-tech industry. Due to his high intelligence, his resourcefulness, and his stock options, he had earned a fortune. At the age of forty-four, he retired. He bought a house on the Mediterranean and a yacht, married a twenty-four-year-old blonde, and started to relax in style. After a few months, however, he was feeling restless instead of relaxed, so he bought himself a vineyard, certain that if he had something to be interested in, he would be fine. But after a year, he grew even more restless. Turns out, he really didn't find the vineyard that interesting. What's more, he was losing interest in the very things he had thought would make him happy: the house, the boat, the lifestyle, even his new wife.

When we started working together, Will immediately wanted to explore the possibility of challenging work, but he was confused about how to go about it. Underlying his confusion was the feeling that it was heresy to doubt the lifestyle of which he had dreamed for so many years, even though it was delivering to him little of what he'd expected.

Professional observations: *Will had to face the fact that, for him, attaining wealth was not the be-all and end-all of his existence but actually the beginning of a new process. He was young, and the same qualities that he had employed to create his financial wealth were still burning brightly. He came to realize he needed to create a new outlet for them. As he did so, he was forced to acknowledge that the value system of our mainstream society is geared toward striving for wealth, not possessing it.*

Consequently, Will was forced to make choices he had never before considered. He came up with a clearer value system for his life than he had ever been aware of, and naturally it led him to new priorities. Once these were in place, the work he wanted to do became evident, and his resourcefulness proved to be a great tool in finding a way to do it.

When I was growing up, I did not work. I didn't baby-sit or mow anyone's lawn for money. In fact, it never occurred to me to work. My father had worked very hard when he was young and had grown up in a family that provided him a great deal of love and loyalty but very little money. My mother didn't work before she finished college. In her family, there was love, loyalty, and a strong work ethic as well, but no expectation for her to work when she was young.

My impression was that my father wanted me to have all of the advantages, privileges, and freedom that he had only dreamed of as a child and had never possessed. In my early adulthood, I had very little awareness of the need to prepare for work or the vital role it would play in my life as an adult. And at first I didn't question this. I simply enjoyed my security and freedom. Looking back, the only thing I ever remember my father saying about work that caused me to reflect on the possibility of one day working myself was that the children of Georgia-Pacific employees were not allowed to work for the company.

So, I blithely pursued my interests: riding horses, studying English literature, learning calligraphy, and traveling, with nary a thought about working for money. Certainly, in many ways, this was enriching, and as I look back on those innocent years, I appreciate the latitude and lack of concern I was given in leading my carefree life. By my early twenties, however, I was already not very good at nurturing relationships with people, even though I had developed a sense that something significant was missing from my life.

One day I went to my father's office and told him I would like to get a job. "Oh, you don't need to work," he replied. "You'll always have enough money to do what you like." Figuring he knew more than I did—though in all honesty I wasn't so cooperative in some other areas of my life—I abandoned the thought of working. For a while, at least. What happened instead was that I started to think of the workaday world as something from which I was excluded.

Eventually, however, I secured some writing jobs, one of them for an equestrian magazine, *Northwest Sporting Horse*. One of the best articles I wrote was a profile on George Morris, who later went on to become the coach of the U.S. Equestrian Team, even though I have to admit the excellence of this piece was due in large part to the fact that he proved to be a very articulate inter-view. To this day I remember many of the things he said during our meeting, such as "Winning has nothing to do with anything but consistency." And he described to me how he stretched riders.

He didn't break them, he said, he *stretched* them. To **"Winning has** this day, that is a principle I have consciously used in **nothing to do** my psychotherapy practice many times.

At that time, however, long before I became a **with anything** psychotherapist, I found that I loved writing about a **but consistency."** sport that was my life. Later, I also enjoyed writing short memorial biographies for a display at Portland's —**George Morris** World Forestry Center. I loved the sense of accomplishment and competence that come from writing creatively, and—drum roll, maestro, please—I loved getting paid! Earning money for the work I had done was an incredibly rich experience. I still find it tremendously exciting and validating.

The transition I made to working as a psychotherapist was immensely logical and natural to me. And though I continued writing occasionally because of the skills I'd acquired, for the first thirty years of my life my real passion was horses. I learned an enormous amount from working with them and navigating the horse world, which for the most part was a relatively safe place where I had developed considerable competence.

Nonetheless, after a while I started to crave the maturity that comes from healthy relationships with people, so I began my passage from the world of horses to the world of people. Near the end of those years with horses, I learned some important lessons while working for Jimmy Kahn in New Hope, Pennsylvania. The focus of his business was re-schooling "problem" horses, and so the transition to working with people's "problems" in psychotherapy proved to include some familiar concepts. I often think how amazing it was that so many of the principles I learned in those many years schooling and training animals apply so aptly to my work with people and how they have proven to be a wonderful introduction and training ground for the work I do now.

There are usually different challenges for the sons of fathers who have made great fortunes than there are for the daughters. For instance, for the sons of tremendously successful businessmen, there can be huge pressure—of which they may not even be conscious—to succeed as largely and importantly in business as their fathers. These sons, therefore, often live with the anxiety and stress of trying to meet the impossibly high standards set by their fathers. Compounding these enormous challenges is the fact that these sons are sometimes arrogant and aloof in their efforts to cover up their insecurities over meeting those standards.

Rarely, too, are these sons humble and articulate about the enormous pressures they are feeling. This is unfortunate because it is impossible, of course, to "measure up" when one considers the unique set of characteristics that contributed to the blastoff success of most of these wealthy fathers: their innate talent, skills, drive, and the prevailing attitudes along with the unique circumstances, timing, and even sheer luck that may have been involved. In fact, the shadow their success casts can be so huge that it spreads darkness across entire generations, from great-great-grandfathers to great-grandfathers to grandfathers and fathers.

It's also sad to say, but true, that these sons and grandsons almost never are able to create that same amount of success. As families' attitudes and behaviors evolve from one generation to the next, the odds against the individual members creating great business success in their lives are heavy. For instance, the odds are *high* that a sense of entitlement and lack of motivation will develop, and *low* that the driving hunger for success and self-discipline to stay focused and make good choices will develop.

Also, they cannot possibly attain the same success because their circumstances are completely different. They are starting out with wealth, education, and an environment that is different from their father's, grandfather's, or other ancestor's, so the incentive to earn can be gone. Yet these sons are typically not inclined to reflect on the formidable obstacles to their own success.

Sadly, too, they often have very little consciousness about their struggle. It would be far wiser for many of them to pursue a different kind of career in art, science, or theology—non-business fields where one is judged entirely on intellect, resourcefulness, and creativity. Here, they are far more likely to achieve self-fulfillment in a world where "dollars earned" is not the primary criterion of success.

Walter Kingsbery, a friend who is an attorney (and not an inheritor), recently took a yearlong sabbatical from his job, during which he gained an awareness of the affirming qualities that his work brings to his life. During his year off, it became clear to Walter that he does not work just for money. In fact, he discovered, one of his primary rewards—purely non-monetary—is the intellectual stimulation he gets from his livelihood. Another is the social interaction he experiences in helping clients resolve dilemmas, along with the keen sense of accomplishment he gets from solving important problems.

"There are days," he concedes, "when I don't like what I'm doing, but now I realize that this is just part of it." He has a rewarding career, he has come to realize, which he appreciates and for which he is grateful, partly because he has learned to hang in there through the tough times.

Certainly, his need to work for money continues to provide the basic motivation that drove him at the beginning of his career and forced him to develop tenacity and resolve to stay the course, no matter what. And now that his practice is well-established, he finds that this ability to stick out the tough times remains a glorious part of it all. Tragically, his is a feeling of competence and achievement that some inheritors will never experience.

Phillip came to me for psychotherapy in his late thirties. He is an inheritor with substantial talent and skills in forensic wildlife biology. When we started working together, he had never been able to sink his teeth into a career, he revealed, because of his reluctance to give up free time and flexibility during the week. He was not afraid of the work, he told me. In fact, he longed for it, but he felt that a forty-hour-a-week commitment would be a self-imposed "straightjacket."

Without such commitment, of course, Phillip could not land a challenging, career-building job. It was a continuing dilemma for him, although his substantial income from inherited wealth made him free to sit on the fence with it. He also knew that practically no one would understand or care about such a dilemma, since the vast majority of people would dearly love to possess both his income and the freedom to contemplate doing anything they wanted.

In addition, his wife, though loving and committed to their marriage, had grown weary and impatient with his struggle, no longer having anything to offer him on this subject but her frustration, so he had stopped trying to discuss the matter with her. And so this had become a private torment for him. His dream was to develop a respectable career as a forensic wildlife biologist, a goal certainly within his grasp were he able and willing to commit to it. When we started working, he felt that his goal might just as well have been to fly to the moon. He was hopelessly grounded, he believed, having already made several attempts at earning graduate degrees and giving up on them too.

Professional observations: Soon after we began working, it became clear to Phillip that in order to realize his dream, he would have to instill the discipline in himself to achieve the career he wanted without the primary motivator: money. He realized with a heavy heart that he could only admire—yes, he went through a period of envy—the motivation for earning money that drives most people and which they take entirely for granted.

Great careers, he came to understand, have been built on the foundation of necessary income. So even though he was reluctant to get off the fence and take his bull, so to speak, firmly by the horns, he decided to use our regular appointments for accountability. I cheered him on and helped him keep the dream alive and his goal in plain sight in front of him. Extremely bright and articulate, Phillip often tried to distract me, but he always allowed me to direct his focus and attention back to his cherished goal. Through hard work, he finally succeeded and now has the career that for years he could only see in his dreams.

Don't invest your time in useless work. For instance, don't move your residence needlessly. It is a waste of time, energy, and money. Many inheritors address their restlessness in this fashion, hoping the novelty of a new house, a different setting, will give them a sense of being in the right place. Usually that restless feeling is an indicator that you are up against the challenge of personal growth in your spirituality, your work, a relationship, or something else important in your life. Don't distract yourself and waste the opportunity to identify and resolve the real cause of your restlessness with the useless work of changing your residence.

Another aspect of work that inheritors often find challenging is acquiring the "street smarts" necessary to compete on equal footing with their co-workers, including bosses and their own employees. Inheritors are sometimes naïve in this regard, due to their growing up in a cushioned world and being used to having their family names and wealth open doors and fix problems for them. Because of this lifelong buffer, inheritors can be slow—even unable—to develop necessary protective instincts to cope with other people's harmful motivations and behaviors.

Phillip had been in his position in forensic wildlife biology for several months when he realized that the lab director harbored many devious qualities potentially detrimental to their professional relationship. Though he had heard other staff members detail this man's negative traits, Phillip was slow to recognize them. Bear in mind that Phillip is bright, but he had brought with him a tendency to assume that the director had the best interests of the lab in mind at all times.

Professional observations: *Phillip had never had to make decisions about work with a superior whose priorities and actions were questionable. Eventually, though, through hard experience, he developed the protective cynicism necessary for the development of his career. Although this is a generalization, inheritors tend to develop this kind of emotional maturity later in life than do non-inheritors.*

Worldly savvy can be a fitful acquisition for inheritors. Developing it is certainly worth the effort though, for its valuable perspective on reality ultimately contributes to the ability to build trust. It is one more important step out of the dark side of wealth.

Gaining Financial Scope

MANY INHERITORS BECOME DISCOURAGED in their early efforts to understand and manage the financial realities of their lives. Men and women experience this phenomenon differently. I think the discouragement for women is related to a weakness in learning mathematics that often manifests itself in fourth or fifth grade when girls, curiously, seem to fall victim to a self-fulfilling prophecy.

Believing at a young age that we can't do well in math, we, of course, don't. Sadly, too, many girls are self-conscious about appearing to be smarter than boys, which can result in a self-fulfilling prophecy of its own, at least in certain areas such as technical proficiency. Now fast-forward a dozen or so years. Unsurprisingly, many young women find they have carried their insecurity in math and technical areas into tentative financial attitudes and lack of competence on an adult level. I was one of them.

For men who feel overwhelmed, it more often comes from the presumption that men understand finance, investments, tax law, etc. Male inheritors may not feel they have permission to ask "stupid questions." Also, men don't have support groups such as Resourceful Women or basic classes such as "Financial Planning for Recent Widows" or "Investment Options for Women." So, where do male inheritors turn to get started? A wealth coach.

In my mid-twenties, I had asked my father to explain investments and tax returns to me. Knowing the kind of person he was, I'm sure he did his best, but in this endeavor we were ships passing in the night. This was extremely frustrating to me, for in my early twenties I had earned a master's degree simply to prove to myself that I could hang in there intellectually with the best of them. I figured I had succeeded. Yet I didn't "get" this financial stuff at all, no matter how hard I tried. Never mind that my postgraduate training was in the liberal arts, I was still deeply discouraged and pushed this feeling of discouragement and a pervading sense of personal deficiency into the background of my life for a while.

A few years passed before I ventured into this painful area again. Finally, I approached my father to ask if I could go over my tax return in detail with our accountant. Yes, of course, he replied, relieved, I'm sure, to relinquish the role of teacher. And so, with great anticipation tinged with nervousness, I went to see the accountant. My excitement, however, soon dissipated as he began explaining *way* over my head. I don't know whether he meant to exclude me totally from our conversation, but that was the effect.

So obscure was his language, he could have been talking in an alien tongue. I doggedly asked questions in a desperate attempt to cull some meaning from his shorthand explanations, but with no success whatsoever. Though hugely discouraged, I finally departed resolved to try again, which I did several times, to no avail. The accountant's words remained foreign to me.

I refused to give up, however. Next, I enrolled in an economics class at a local university and stuck with it the whole term, only to wind up more intimidated than ever. "This *cannot* be impossible for me to understand!" I kept thinking, hoping for a breakthrough. But it never came. I simply couldn't get anywhere. At times I seemed to grasp a small piece of the puzzle, but then I wasn't able to fit it into the overall picture. Or I couldn't retain the clarity of my scraps of comprehension. Or I would hear something else that contradicted the information I thought I understood. Still, I clung to a growing desire for responsibility for my own financial affairs.

I persisted in my resolve by talking with stockbrokers and even made a few tentative investments, but none of that helped. I remained at the starting line in my quest for financial enlightenment, by then so intimidated that my mind would shut down— literally go blank—whenever I tried to focus on any of the numbers or concepts I had packed into my brain. And though it all struck me as extremely strange at the time, I now know that this self-induced mental haze is fairly common among female inheritors. Indeed, I've often heard this alarming phenomenon discussed in my private practice and workshops.

Elena told me she had a trust fund which was run by "three trustees who work for my father." She said that she has access to the trust fund and, in fact, thinks she doesn't spend all she's entitled to. She was just awakening to the beginning of her journey to financial responsibility and said, "I can understand financial matters when my older sister explains them to me. When my father explains, I go into a glaze. He likes to explain and he's open about his businesses, but I can't really hear it."

Professional observations: *It is common for inheritors in the early stages of understanding their inheritance to go into a "glaze." The language and the concepts both can be overwhelming. Many inheritors have the reaction of going into a fog or daydreaming during meetings and explanations. Often they also feel guilty and ashamed about their inability to pay attention.*

Looking back, I gratefully credit my mother for her gifts to me in my struggle for financial competence: energy, determination, and stamina. These strengths, among others, that she instilled in me have held me in good stead through many challenges. In the monumental task of confronting the financial realities of my life, the resolve to succeed led me eventually to an exceptional financial planner. Had I not persisted in my determination and efforts, I might never have found her. I had arrived at the real beginning of my journey.

Financial planners, by the very nature of their work, can be excellent tutors, as proficient at sketching the big picture as they are in delineating the details. This remarkable planner promptly dedicated herself to working with my husband and me together. With the instinctual skills of a true teacher she simplified the language, principles, and concepts for us, assigned learning projects and homework, and painstakingly began laying out the building blocks of our financial education.

A financial planner can also be a good resource in securing the expertise of other professionals when needed, e.g., accountants, investment managers, bankers, attorneys, etc., though it's important to pay financial planners for their *services* only and not for *products* they help you acquire. Not everyone needs a financial planner, but it's a good idea to find out whether or not you do need one early rather than late. If you decide to enlist the services of such a professional, do your best to find one who specializes in or has experience in the area of inherited wealth.

Either a financial planner or an estate-planning attorney can help you get oriented to legal issues that concern you and your financial assets, including trusts, wills, asset protection, estate-tax minimization, and life-insurance needs. You will want to start with anything that has been created specifically for you, typically by older-generation family members. As heirs age, more assets often come to them outright, which is why it becomes important for inheritors to take control and be able to make educated decisions in regard to their finances.

When she first came to see me, Liv was forty-six, newly separated from her husband of twenty years, and slowly grasping the grim reality that over the past few years he had lost her entire inheritance, which had come to her in lump sums during the settlement of her parents' estates. A bright, attractive woman who had drifted into a relationship full of denial and deceit, she had been relieved to let him deal with all of their financial concerns, believing everything to be fine—as it always had been in her untrammeled life.

She had known that several of his businesses had failed, but she thought, perhaps too willingly, that his failures had been offset by his successes. Resolutely, she now realized, she had kept her head stuck firmly in the sand, content not to think or worry about such mundane matters, reassured by his charming and confident manner. Not until she met with a financial planner, much too late, did she learn the disastrous consequences of her blithe aloofness. It was the financial planner who quickly realized what had happened and helped establish some protective limits. Her next step was to send Liv to me.

Professional observations: *The density of Liv's denial was immediately striking to me, and it is surprisingly common among female inheritors. Often, wealthy little girls are brought up to believe that all financial concerns are "taken care of" at Daddy's office, and when these girls grow up and marry, it is the path of least resistance to continue to expect to be benevolently taken care of. It is a nice fantasy, and once in a while it works out fine, but often the results of this hands-off attitude are disastrous, as in Liv's case.*

As you start to become educated in working with professional advisors to handle the legal and financial concerns that affect you, you will progress into doing your estate planning. Typically, one of the first steps in your own planning is to create a will. Although thinking about your death may be difficult, clarifying the plans for your estate in a will is a kind, considerate, and responsible act. What's more, it affords you the opportunity to be creative and inspired in your estate planning.

For instance, you may decide to create an incentive trust for your children, a "cause-and-effect trust," as Myra Salzer, a Boulder, Colorado, financial planner likes to call it. This sort of trust provides young beneficiaries the opportunity to learn more about your personal values by interacting with a plan set up to teach and impart these values through experience and reward.

Financial planners like to do financial projections, and you may find these fascinating, scary, or both. At the very least, it will be interesting for you to discover what happens when you alter your spending habits so that you can ratchet them up or down with an eye, say, toward living to the ripe old age of 120, or in anticipation of interest rates changing drastically, or even considering the eventuality of protracted market corrections.

With a planner you can study all the possible ways that these projections might affect your options, using the various financial scenarios to be intentional about your present and future lifestyles as well as to set goals for the signposts of your life. Working with a planner is a great place to start your financial education and to begin "integrating" with your assets.

If your wealth is inherited, its protection will be one of your first concerns. You will want to ensure sound management and growth because you can't make up the loss. You may consider buying insurance, and you will probably find that at different times of your life, different kinds and amounts of insurance are important. Your financial planner or another financial or legal professional can refer you to a reputable insurance agent or can recommend "no-load" insurance. Because of the constantly evolving estate-tax environment and possible law changes, it is best to review your insurance needs regularly.

Irrevocable trusts are often used to protect financial assets, and many kinds are available. You can tailor a trust in just about any way you wish. All trusts involve three parties: the benefactor (grantor), the beneficiary (grantee), and the trustee. Trusts are written for a specific term of existence, usually one or two generations beyond the grantor, and once the trust is signed into effect, the benefactor and beneficiary typically have little power to influence the duties of the trustee.

Generally, a trustee is responsible for prudence, diversification, and looking after the best interests of the primary (income) beneficiary(ies) and/or the secondary (principal) beneficiary(ies). Irrevocable trusts can provide excellent protection against lawsuits. There is a price, however, to be paid for this protection. One price is the grantor's loss of ownership and control over the assets in the trust.

Another price involves the complexity of the resulting administrative requirements. If you are given any role in a trust, you will need to become oriented to exactly what it demands of you, for your responsibility will be to function as efficiently and productively as possible in order to serve everyone (including yourself) well. A primary challenge of inheritors is to develop an understanding of the nature of the wealth for which they are responsible. Only through this knowledge and competency will they be able to steward it for their sake and the sake of their heirs.

In the case of a trust, investment management of trust assets is the responsibility of the trustee. However, investment management of your assets is your responsibility. One of the first requisites of asset protection, therefore, is the precise definition of one's financial "nut," i.e., the amount the inheritor will need to support his or her standard of living. The rest, considered "discretionary," is available for spending, philanthropy, gifting, and/or increasing the "nut." You may decide that only the nut needs to be assiduously guarded, or you may decide to take stewardship of all of it very much to heart. Certainly you can hire management firms and consultants to do this for you (for instance, stocks, bonds, and real estate can all be handled by hired managers), but it is *your* responsibility to oversee their work, for one simple reason: It is *your* money, and therefore your gain or your loss.

All of this means that you have to understand your options and boundaries and the rules that pertain to the assets over which you have control. You need to know who is responsible for what and how everything works in regard to your financial goals. There are many books, courses, and seminars available to you to achieve these ends. One great resource for this education is *Winning the Loser's Game,* by Charles D. Ellis. Or you may choose to acquire your education directly from your investment manager or financial planner. Do this simply by paying close attention and listening to *everything* being told to you. Each time you have a question—the simpler the better—*ask* it, no matter how elementary or dumb you think it may sound.

Take the following definitions. These are financial terms you need to understand clearly. If you find them difficult to focus on or to comprehend fully, a good place to start would be to ask a financial professional to help you with them.

What is stock? A stock is simply a share (or shares) in a company. By purchasing stock, you become a part owner in that company. When the value of your stock goes up, you can sell it and make money. When the value of your stock goes down, you can lose money by selling it for less than you originally paid. The key, sometimes much easier said than done, is to sell your stock at a higher price than you bought it for.

What are bonds? Bonds are issued by corporations or federal or local government entities for the purpose of borrowing money to fund a project (such as a hospital wing or bridge reconstruction). When you buy a bond, you are loaning money to the issuer of that bond. Bonds pay their owners regular interest, usually twice a year. Many people use this interest income for spending.

What are cash equivalents? Simply put, cash equivalents are places for you to hold your money while you are waiting to invest or spend it. Cash equivalents are "liquid," meaning you can get hold of the money quickly and without penalty, usually within a day or two of your decision to do something different with it. There is lower risk and more certainty involved because the amount you get out will be very close to what you put in compared to other types of investments. Examples of cash equivalents are money-market funds, certificates of deposit, and short-term treasuries.

What is real estate? As an investment, real estate is considered to be excellent and lucrative by some, and too risky or illiquid and difficult to value by others. All would agree, however, on two points: (1) expertise is critical in the handling of real-estate investments and (2) real estate is not liquid and therefore is a long-term venture.

Other than some alternative investments (e.g., commodities and hedge funds), the answers to the four questions above pretty much cover the range of investment territory. This said, any financial planner will quickly add that researching investments and reaching decisions about them are complex endeavors. Basic answers to simple questions are given here as a starting point for inheritors in becoming oriented and organizing their thinking in regard to difficult but necessary matters. This is the kind of terrain you will need to tread in your quest for financial scope.

Remember, too, that financial professionals have their own language, as do experts in any field. Keep in mind that their jargon is so familiar to them they may not realize they are using words and concepts totally foreign to you. Therefore, you have to bring to the table the attitude that *every* time something comes up about investment management which you don't fully understand, ask a simple question such as "What *is* that?" or "What are you talking about?" If your financial professional cannot or will not answer these questions to your satisfaction, find one who will. Remember that he or she is working for *you*, not the other way around. It's that simple.

Once you gain a foothold in your understanding of investments and financial management, you can begin to participate in multi-generational planning for your family. You will have confidence and worthwhile questions to ask. Multi-generational planning includes children, grandchildren, parent, and grandparent relationships. Often family business entities, such as LLCs (limited liability companies) and FLPs (family limited partnerships) are used. These can be complex, but go ahead and ask your questions. They will help everyone clarify their thoughts.

Evelyn, age sixty-one, has been married for forty years. Her husband has just retired from his job as an automobile corporation executive. Evelyn's brother, Isaac, has been managing the family finances for the past thirty years. This arrangement began following the death of Evelyn's father, who in his will relegated this authority to Isaac. In turn, Isaac has been benevolent and has given Evelyn money for years, but no information.

In fact, Isaac has recently set up a family limited partnership with Evelyn and their mom. Evelyn has no idea what this is, even though she is a member of it. She has grown uncomfortable with her position of being taken care of in the dark. Partly this is due to her brother's secrecy and partly because she and her husband have begun to feel that Isaac may be hiding something from them. She has started asking for information but is not yet receiving any.

Professional observations: This sort of arrangement is quite common. Sometimes the brother (uncle, cousin) is doing a good job, but sometimes not. Ultimately it is up to each individual to take responsibility for his or her own finances. And it can be a lot of work to get information and make sense of it. Without this step of maturity, an inheritor remains childlike.

Once it has occurred to you to ask questions and become informed, persist in your efforts. By doing so, you are taking charge of your financial life. I often help clients clarify their thoughts into assertive statements. Assertiveness is the midpoint on a continuum:

| Aggression | Assertiveness | Passivity |

Aggression and passivity are far more common behaviors than assertiveness. Furthermore, many people confuse assertiveness with aggression. The ability to be assertive is a powerful tool. In being assertive, we know we are true to ourselves in speaking up about what we believe. Also, when we make an assertive statement instead of an aggressive or passive statement, we are most likely to be heard. The preparation of an assertive statement can and should be approached in a methodical manner.

Each step can be worked out on paper as it applies to the situation in which you want to be assertive, and invariably it is easy to see the effectiveness of this approach. Following is an example of an assertive statement that a client developed for herself to use with her cousin Jeff. She, Jeff, and several more relatives are shareholders in a large multi-location group of businesses. Jeff is president of the entire group, some of whom, including my client, are board members. Jeff has a history of being uncooperative with all the family members. She used this statement with him on the phone, although it would have been as effective in person or in writing.

I have not received a response from you to my letter about sending me timely monthly distributions and monthly financial reports as dictated by our by-laws. You did make a quarterly distribution at the end of the year, and in the past you have sent me annual reports. When you don't respond to my letters, I feel ignored and worried that you didn't receive them. I would like you to respond to my letters, and I would like monthly distributions and financial reports. Because you've been cooperative by having Deloitte and Touche talk to my accountant, I feel you probably received my letter and were responding to some extent. This gives me confidence that we will be able to work this out.

There are many ways to transfer assets and income. In addition to LLCs and FLPs, other financial tools could involve the outright gifting of cash, 529 college savings plans, and UGMA custodial accounts. Only through clear educated thinking can you make wise choices that will reap far-reaching benefits to you and your loved ones.

In the course of making these financial choices, sooner or later the subject of philanthropy will occur to you. Your first thoughts about giving away some of your wealth may come in response to a request from a charitable organization. Or, on your own, you may notice a need in the world and feel inspired to help. As you become inspired, you may enter a period of self-examination as to whether philanthropy represents a moral obligation, an opportunity for personal growth, or both.

At this juncture, you will probably begin to wonder, "How much can I afford to give?" and "What is the best way for me to use my wealth to help others?" Many people start with direct gifts of time, talent, or treasure. Some give all three. Your values, priorities, and availability will guide you in making your choices.

Whether or not you have established a strong charitable relationship with an organization, school, church, or community, you may decide to create a private family foundation, a charitable remainder trust, or a legacy gift to benefit those where you see the need most clearly. In these philanthropic responses there may be tax benefits for you. Always keep your motives in giving clear so that you can accomplish your goals.

As the inheritor explores his or her philanthropic course of action, many really hit their stride in regard to their sense of purpose in the world. Philanthropy is known for rewarding our generosity in this way. People who have thrown their hearts and souls—and whatever money they could afford—into charitable causes will tell you that the emotional and spiritual rewards are many times greater than what they put in and can be the bearers of delightful surprises. The only way to understand this is to experience it.

For the inheritor, tax preparation and planning are endeavors that usually require the professional services of a certified public accountant.

When Maiya graduated from college in 1980, she was ready to grab the brass ring of life. When she told her father, the founder and owner of a multibillion-dollar complex of businesses head-quartered on the East Coast, that she was moving to San Francisco, he told her curtly, "If you do, I'll cut you off."

"Fine," Maiya replied, "I can support myself," and off she went. Bright and conscientious, she found a position soon after her move to the distant city but immediately realized she would not be able to support herself on her salary. So she got another job and another and another, four in all. The following January, when she received the W-2's from her employers, she diligently computed her taxes and, with great personal satisfaction, filed her first return.

Meanwhile, unbeknownst to Maiya, her father's accountant had filed another return for her that included transactions and income involving the assets her father had placed in her name but had never told her about. Subsequently, her father's accountant received a letter from the IRS questioning his complicated return that conflicted with hers. Soon after, she heard from her highly chagrined father. "How could you do this to me?" he demanded. "Do you realize the havoc you've created by attracting the attention of the IRS?"

"What's the problem?" asked Maiya, completely bewildered. "I worked, got my W-2's, filed my return, and paid my taxes. How did it affect you?"

Professional observations: *Some creators of wealth view life as a chess game. Maiya's independent behavior took her out of her father's control, and he found out too late that it would have been a* *good idea to inform his daughter of her status and involvement in his financial affairs. The financial education of inheritors needs to start at a young age and progress in age-appropriate stages from the early years of allowances and instruction concerning spending, saving, and the giving away of money. Only in this open, trusting way will parents and children each benefit from their family wealth, both given and received.*

Clearly, Maiya's parents had provided her with some excellent parenting. They had raised a daughter who was conscientious, responsible, a self-starter, and well-educated. If they had only educated her regarding her own financial situation, she would have come into young adulthood with some financial maturity. In this example, the problem resides not with Maiya but with her dad.

If you have a financial planner, he or she can coordinate tax preparation and planning for you. If, instead, you work directly with an investment manager, he or she may provide this coordination or can work with your accountant to plan for and prepare tax returns. The vast majority of wealthy people use these professional services, and any one of them can help you build your team.

In summing up, I acknowledge that many important and complex financial considerations are merely touched upon in this chapter and require much more exploration and education on your part. Please don't be discouraged! Begin at the beginning and take one step at a time. Allow yourself to go forward in baby steps and give yourself permission to make some mistakes. Remember that even the most savvy financial geniuses probably knew as little as you do when they were just beginning. Remind yourself that you can be just as competent as you need to be if you decide to take on the challenge.

If you don't have a family member whom you trust and who is knowledgeable and skilled in teaching financial concerns, then hire a suitable professional with your need for education in mind. Or take a course to get yourself started. Also, there are excellent, elementary books on financial subjects. You can gain the expertise you need to track your financial team and make wise decisions. Keep firmly in mind that you don't have to do it alone. The benefits to you of finding ways to stand on your own and rely on yourself are financial health and emotional maturity.

All you have to do is ask. And ask. And ask again.

The Value of Estate Planning

MANY OF THE LEGAL ISSUES with which an inheritor needs to be concerned involve estate planning. You may not be aware of it, but you have an estate plan. Upon your death, if you have not created legal documents to specifically address the plan, the state in which you reside has done it for you. Without your own documents, it will be the *state* that determines who receives your assets when you die, not *you*. The way this is set up by the state is *generally* what many people want, but most people would prefer to control the distribution of their estates directly through a will, which overrides state law. It is the process of preparation of this vital document that often serves as the catalyst for an inheritor to seek my counsel.

When Margaret first came to see me, her attorney had relegated the drafting of her will to the background of his attention. After telling him what she wanted her will to say, Margaret had altered her specifications several times and had become so hesitant in signing the document that he felt frustrated and baffled. To all outward appearances, she seemed to have become intimidated by the process of formalizing the disposition of her estate.

When this happens, experience has shown me that ugly emotions usually lie buried just beneath the surface, emotions that the person who is struggling with a will is often not very aware of. As Margaret shared her personal history with me, it was easy for me as an outsider to guide her to the area of her life that was troubling and hindering her.

Her deceased husband, Don, had been a wealthy man and had bequeathed most of his financial assets to her. Their marriage was the second for both of them, and he had died less than two years afterwards, survived by two grown children from his first marriage. Margaret had three grown children from her own first marriage.

While one of them, her oldest son, was doing "pretty well," in her words, the other two were not. Her second son, a stonemason, was capable of doing good work but was not much of a businessman, she revealed. He had "worked hard but not smart" and had failed to build any sort of equity from his career. Her youngest child, a daughter divorced from an abusive marriage, was now putting all of her energy into raising her children and barely making ends meet. Don's two sons, on the other hand, were doing very well, she told me. Both owned a business and were making enough money to support privileged lifestyles for themselves and their families.

At first, Margaret had thought she would divide the wealth equally five ways, but after creating a will that stipulated these provisions and then mulling over other ideas as well, she found herself at an impasse on what to do. A complicating factor was that Don had left her a "modest" rather than lavish fortune with the assets unsheltered from taxes. Another problem for Margaret was that when she was in her twenties, her grandfather had died suddenly and somehow—she was unclear exactly how—everything of value had gone to her uncle.

Now in her mid-sixties, she had carried that pain of being "left out" for forty years, she said, relating her mother's sadness as well. Now, she told me, she wanted her will to correct that "wrong," but she wanted to do the right thing for the children as well. Through a lengthy and admittedly painful exploration of her priorities and values, Margaret finally reached clarity over exactly what it was she wanted to accomplish with her will. She came up with a plan which she felt was truly fair. She told her attorney, he wrote up the will accordingly, and she promptly signed it.

Professional observations: Margaret felt ashamed of the painful "hurt" feelings she had carried with her since her twenties. She felt immature every time she realized she was thinking about those days so long ago. She was struggling with the challenge of wanting to leave equal shares to each of the five adult children, yet considering their financial circumstances, was that really fair? In order to solve her impasse, she had to work her way through the thoughts and emotions she associated with the concept that what is fair is not necessarily what is equal. With courage and repeated focus, she accomplished her task.

As an inheritor, you may find yourself the beneficiary of a trust agreement. This is a common estate-planning tool and has been for decades. Being a beneficiary simply means you are designated in the trust agreement as someone who benefits from it. The benefactor (also referred to as the settlor or grantor) is the person (or one of the persons) who created the trust and put assets into it. Basically, here's how it works.

Let's say I have a specific amount of material wealth, which I would like to give to you. Let's say these assets consist of stocks, bonds, an office building, and a diamond ring. I want you to have them but not until you're fifty years old, so I'm going to have Joe Smith take care of them for you until then. Through a trust agreement, I'm going to set up rules for him to follow until your fiftieth birthday. He is the trustee. I am the benefactor. You are the beneficiary.

Having said this, I must quickly add that there are many different kinds of trust agreements, but every trust is either revocable or irrevocable. *Revocable* means that under certain circumstances, the benefactor has the power to change or dissolve it. Revocable trusts typically are used for purposes of asset management, probate avoidance, or privacy. Generally, a revocable trust becomes irrevocable at the death of the creator.

Irrevocable means that the person creating the trust may *not* dissolve it and probably retains very little power to change anything else about the trust. Almost every trust is created and governed by a written trust agreement, about which the beneficiary has a legal right to acquire at least some information. The right to obtain a copy of the trust document varies by state. For instance, a beneficiary may have the right to learn the terms of the trust that affect his or her interests but may not have the right to secure a copy of the entire document.

Be sure to request and read all of the information to which you have legal access. If there's anything you don't understand on your own (which there almost certainly will be), find an attorney, make an appointment, and ask him or her to explain it to you. There are many smart, kind, and unfailingly attentive trustees in the world. If you're blessed with one, you can exercise your gratitude and express your compliments and appreciation for the excellent work being done on your behalf. Keep in mind, however, that there are other trustees who fall far short of doing a great job, some to the point of inflicting significant financial harm on their clients. Make sure you know which of the two is shepherding your interests.

If you're not sure, start asking questions. Immediately. You may even need to enlist another professional to help you investigate. You must pay *attention* and take full responsibility for seeing that your trust is being wisely and proficiently attended to by your trustee. No one else will—or *should*—do this for you. To put it bluntly, it is immature and foolish to blithely ignore your trusts and/or trustees. If you don't presently want the income from the trust, you may be able to direct it back into the principal of the trust or be allowed to give the money to a charity. It is your responsibility to make the situation work for you.

One of the first clients to come to me with wealth issues was Ann, a widow in her early sixties. Her attorney had referred her because she, too, had reached an impasse in her estate planning. Both Ann and her lawyer recognized her dilemma, and she wanted to be thorough in working her way through it, so he suggested that she do it with me.

Ann had three grown children, whose individual circumstances and life-coping abilities differed markedly from each other. The oldest daughter was a "spendthrift" who had accumulated a great deal of possessions (houses, cars, boats, horses, and luxuries of all kinds), Ann told me. The middle child, a son, was institutionalized with a serious mental disorder and deemed incapable of living on his own. Her younger son, a successful businessman with a large income, had married his high school sweetheart and had a stable family life.

Like Margaret, Ann originally had wanted to divide the estate equally among her heirs but soon decided this was not the best plan since the children differed so much in competency from each other. Though she had moved on to considering a combination of outright gifts and trusts, she was nonetheless immobilized by her determination to make everything "equal" for them.

Her daughter objected to a trust despite her mother's strong feelings that it would be in her best interests, providing her an opportunity to mature in her attitude toward money before she frivolously spent it all. A trust was clearly the best choice for her institutionalized middle son as well. Her younger son, on the other hand, had long demonstrated his competency in handling his finances and his life; for him, she felt, a trust would not be appropriate. After much careful consideration, Ann settled on a combination of planning entities for each heir, which she came to see as fair though not equal.

Professional observations: *As it is in life, so it is in estate planning. Ann had already experienced many years of shielding her children's differences from each other. Once she worked out the plan she wanted for each of her adult children, we role-played each of their various possible reactions and how she could handle them well.*

There are many other kinds of trusts that may affect you as a beneficiary or which you may choose to use in the estate planning you do for your heirs. Some of the irrevocable trusts common to inheritance are incentive trusts (a type of trust usually set up for the transfer of assets to children), marital trusts, charitable trusts, and credit shelter, family, or "bypass" trusts. Your attorney can explain any that affect you or any in which you are interested.

Bear firmly in mind, though, that some attorneys, despite possessing excellent professional skills, may not be good teachers. If, after talking with your attorney, you feel that you still don't have a firm grasp of the estate-planning concepts you are trying to understand and their potential implications on your financial future or that of your heirs, *tell* him or her. If necessary, ask for help in finding someone who can better explain the financial effects of chosen legal vehicles. Be persistent in your determination to educate yourself. You can understand it all fully if you will just dig.

Many inheritors become intimidated or bored by legal and financial considerations and concerns, with sometimes tragic consequences. If you are hampered by such emotions, again I say *persist.* If you will just sustain your efforts to understand, ask as many questions as necessary of your advisors, and keep re-asking if necessary, you *will* succeed, I promise you. In so doing, beyond attaining the understanding that is so vital to your future, you will also build the confidence that comes from refusing to relinquish your goals. The greater the struggle, the dearer the prize called maturity that you can only win for yourself, for no amount of money can buy it for you.

Inheritors who are married or engaged may have specific concerns regarding the legal rights and agreements associated with their union. No doubt, the most-publicized marital contract is the prenuptial agreement. Commonly, this is a legal agreement designed to address the disposition of the financial assets of both spouses upon divorce or the death of either spouse. Granted, the consideration and resolution of a prenuptial agreement is possibly the most unromantic activity an engaged couple can undertake. Nevertheless, given the climate of divorce in our society and the certainty (except in rare cases) that one spouse will die before the other, considering a prenuptial agreement may be a wise premarital endeavor.

As in the case of wills, there are state laws that address rights to financial assets upon the divorce of any couple or the death of a spouse in that state. Here, too, your own prenuptial agreement (or marital agreement if written after the marriage has taken place) will override state law. Generally these marriage-related contracts are straightforward and commonsensical and most people can understand them easily. Once in a while, however, I hear about an unusual variation.

Whitney and her husband, Scott, both in their late twenties, had been married for three years and had a six-month-old daughter when they came in to see me. Despite the baby and their sincere efforts to make a happy life for themselves, they were not getting along well. Scott was from a working-class background, Whitney revealed, and his life experiences had been a world apart from hers. It became quickly evident that their values were very different and that their opposing priorities were straining the marriage.

After a few sessions, it occurred to Whitney to tell me about their prenuptial agreement, which her father, a wealthy man in a distant city, and his attorney had written for them. It stipulated that, in the event of a divorce, her husband would receive $100,000 for every year they were married. "So I've already made it to $300,000!" Scott interrupted, and though his remark seemed lighthearted, I did not get the impression he was joking at all, particularly when he went on to point out, "And if I stay for ten years, it's a million dollars."

"But then that's it," Whitney interjected. "However long we stay together after that, the money he gets stays at a million."

Now, as a therapist, it is one of my responsibilities to remain neutral emotionally, but this revelation tested me. I found I had to set aside my immediate thoughts and reactions and keep my focus entirely on Whitney and Scott, for they clearly needed help at this point.

Professional observations: *Undoubtedly, someone had good intentions in creating this prenuptial agreement, but the result was not conducive or constructive to anyone's mental health. This young couple had many challenges, and Whitney's inheritance was only one of them. I helped them do their work on finding values and priorities in common, and they built on that.*

Certainly, many legal concerns exist for inheritors in the area of family businesses and/or investment entities. Sometimes these are connected, sometimes they are independent. A popular estate-planning tool currently involves use of a business entity called a limited liability company (LLC) or another called a family limited partnership (FLP). Here's how they work.

Typically, the senior member of a family has the most financial assets. Concluding that more of his estate than he would like will be going into paying taxes after his death, he decides to set up a business entity into which he places certain financial assets. Let's say he puts stocks and real estate into the LLC. He chooses several in particular that he expects to increase in value over the coming years. An appraiser then values the interests in the business entity holding these assets.

The asset valuations are, in fact, discounted by the appraiser because of the form of the entity that holds them. Family members buy or are given "units" of the LLC, and the wealth can be transferred essentially at a discount. Many restrictions apply, and the structure of the LLC or FLP can be complicated, but their use now in estate planning is widespread.

The lesson is this: Ask questions until you fully and clearly understand the LLC or the FLP being set up, exactly how it involves you, and how it affects you now and in the future. For though the estate-tax benefits may be immediately apparent, what could also happen upon the death of the person creating the LLP or FLP are possible legal entanglements with siblings or other family members who do not have your best interests at heart.

Inheritors are likely to find that they have legal concerns regarding charitable giving. There are many ways to give money to others, and one of the reasons the choices exist involves tax benefits. Sometimes a wealthy individual will choose to create a private foundation. A private charitable foundation can make it possible for financial gifts to go to recipients without calling attention to the individual who has provided the money. Another reason for creating a charitable foundation is that you can put the money in now, get the tax benefits now, and yet take years to decide where the vast majority of the money will go.

Legally the foundation will be required to grant or give a minimum of 5 percent of its asset-value per year. A private charitable foundation can be of any size. It could be started with ten dollars, but you should target funding of at least $250,000 or the administrative costs will be too high. Sometimes a wealthy individual will create a charitable remainder trust. Under this structure, the charitable beneficiary may receive nothing for years until after the death of the benefactor, and the benefactor receives cash flow from the trust during his or her lifetime. In this case, there are tax benefits both during the benefactor's lifetime and after his or her death.

There are various kinds of asset-protection structures set up by wealthy individuals and inheritors. LLCs, FLPs, and trusts have some asset-protection benefits. Retirement accounts can be included here. The "Alaska Trust" and the "Delaware Trust" are two that are typically used for asset protection, as well as "off shore" trusts.

The applicable exclusion amount is an allowance the government makes for giving money free of estate taxes. Each person has a lifetime exclusion (this refers to money you can give away free of estate taxes), which, for example, is $1 million for 2003. You can use your exclusion to make gifts at any time or times during your life or at death, and you can divide it up in many ways. This $1 million is scheduled to increase periodically up to $3.5 million in 2009. The rules regarding estate tax are in a state of flux. They are being revised, challenged, and rethought constantly by members of Congress. This is an area, therefore, in which the only wise approach is to consult with your professional advisors on an ongoing basis to find out how these rules apply to you in the present.

In conclusion, since many of the circumstances and techniques relevant to estate planning are in flux, your attorney and your financial planner play important roles in guiding you on how to use the laws well. It is their responsibility to know and to understand the law, and they can help you address all of your planning issues.

Through the Eye of a Needle

THE GREATEST CHALLENGE OF WEALTH is spiritual: You have been given much, so you have the opportunity to respond richly. This is made clear in the biblical story of the talents in Matthew 25:14–30 that describes the choices we have to optimize God's gifts.

When we begin to believe in God, we become aware of the responsibility that goes along with the blessings God gives us. We have to ask ourselves, "What am I going to *do* with this abundance God has placed in my life?" We need to ask *because* of our abundance, because of the great variety of opportunities for both good and bad choices this abundance presents to us, and because many paths of folly are available to the inheritor. In contrast, the paths of wisdom are few and harder to travel. The spiritual challenge of wealth, therefore, establishes what your life is about and what you will or will not accomplish with your abundance.

The world's great religions teach that material wealth is not conducive to spiritual strength, as evidenced by the single passage in the Bible that provided me with the seed for this book: "And Jesus said to His disciples, 'Truly I say to you, it is hard for a rich person to enter the kingdom of heaven. And again I say to you, it

> The greatest challenge of wealth is spiritual: You have been given much, so you have the opportunity to respond richly.

is easier for a camel to go through the eye of a needle than for a rich person to enter the kingdom of God'" (Matthew 19:23–24).

One of the main problems, not only for inheritors but for virtually everyone in our society, is that material wealth is so beguiling. It usurps our attention, dominates our time, and seduces our affection. We all have the same finite amount of time in our day, and what we choose to give our attention to shows us where our hearts are. What each of us does with our precious time reveals what we love. It's that simple.

My Christian commitment has been evident throughout my writing. Equally apparent, I hope, is my inclusive attitude, for my main objective is to awaken in readers the desire to turn increasing attention to their spiritual lives, to prioritize God in their existence if they have not done so already. God honors our desire to draw close: "I love those who love me; and those who diligently seek me will find me" (Proverbs 8:17).

Most religious and spiritual paths instruct that their way of seeking and worship is the only way to know God. I know that God is just (John 5:30), and God alone will judge our paths of worship. I encourage you, therefore, if you are presently asleep at the wheel of your spiritual life, to begin your journey to know God in ways with which *you* are familiar and by studying things about God in which *you* are curious. However you seek, though, be certain of one thing: If you open your eyes to God in your life, you *will* be rewarded.

⌒

In our culture, material wealth is typically perceived to be solid, trustworthy security we can always count on. Certainly, material needs that have been well met do make us feel secure, and material comforts are, indeed, pleasing. And thus, material wealth has seductive power. Under close scrutiny, however, the inherent problems of placing our faith in material wealth become evident. True security is not dependent on material well-being. When people lose their financial footing, which sometimes happens, they often lose their feeling of security as well. So that kind of "security" isn't real in the first place.

Material wealth has seductive power.

Genuine well-being does not fade or change in negative ways at the diminishment of financial security. For example, the new house you moved into, which provided you with such an exhilarating sense of security, turned out to harbor unanticipated challenges to that security. How did that happen? Because it wasn't real security in the first place.

Another measure of true security is its inherent foothold in one's life. Once you truly possess it, it is simply there. No effort is needed to preserve or enhance it. It is a part of who you are, despite the subsequent loss of material wealth, should that be your misfortune. In other words, financial well being does *not* assure general well-being, despite the popular conception that it does.

People who possess material wealth usually battle with a sense of selfishness over it. Before making material or cash gifts, an inevitable thought process ensues to ensure that the gift will not diminish one's wealth to the point of psychological pain. "Giving till it hurts," in the jargon of charity fund-raisers, is not something the wealthy do willingly. The paradox here is that true security is not a finite substance. It is actually enhanced when it is shared.

Think of a candle flame as representing your security. Someone else comes up with an unlit candle. You say, "Here, I'll share my security with you," and you light his candle with your flame. As a result, your flame is still the same, but you can see the additional brightness in the world from sharing your gift. This symbolism of the flame doesn't work with material wealth because it's a finite substance, and if you shared yours, you would have less.

The point is that philanthropy—the sharing of material wealth—can have a place in spiritual security as long as one's focus is squarely on the spiritual values involved. This focus, however, is extremely difficult to achieve. Few people of means succeed in maintaining it.

If, however, you own no financial wealth—if you are poor— where to base your emotional security is a different matter. Poor people more often seek their emotional security by turning to their spiritual rather than financial resources for the obvious reason that the latter option is not available to them. Rich people, on the other hand, can go either way, as difficult as the choice may be, because society steadfastly encourages us to place our sense of security primarily in material rather than spiritual wealth. Life is complicated no matter who you are.

As an inheritor attempting to develop your spiritual life, you will soon discover that the guiding principles in achieving security are literally upside down from the standpoint of widespread secular understanding. That is why the spiritual journey is not for the timid or the weak.

⌣

Whatever blessings we find in our journey through life, God intends for us to use them to bless others as well. For each of us, the quality of our relationship with God will be affected by what we do with God's gifts to us. Sometimes this involves a large measure of risk. In Genesis 12:1–5, God calls Abram from his comfortable home and life in Haran to go out and be a blessing to others. Abram and his wife, Sarai, had become very much at ease in their lives and their community. They were minding their own business and busy meeting life's daily challenges, as most of us are, when God summoned Abram to *significance*, telling him to "Go! And be a blessing to others!"

God instructed Abram to leave everything he had come to count on for his emotional and material security and to trust and let God be his guide. Abram had no idea where his cooperation with God would lead him. He had no idea that the Messiah would be descended from him and that for countless thousands of years he would be seen as a guiding example of the power of man when yielding to God's will.

God may also call on *you*, and this journey may put you into risk you can't even imagine handling. But God blesses us when we stretch ourselves, and the risks you will take will strengthen your faith and lead you to more blessings. That is God's assurance.

When I was just twelve, I watched my mother pack her suitcase and leave on a mission trip to Lambarene in French Equatorial Africa (now Gabon), to help Dr. Albert Schweitzer in his hospital there. In yielding to God's will she stepped out of her comfortable and familiar life. She knew little about how she would be called to help once there. Yet aside from the assistance she provided in Africa, she also inspired many others at home. Recently, over four decades after her Lambarene trip, a child-hood friend of mine approached us one day when we were together and thanked my mother for having spoken to our seventh-grade class about her trip. She thanked her for her stimulating words that day so long ago and added that because of her visit to our class she, too, has harbored the desire to make such a trip. She told us with clear delight that hers was now planned and that she was leaving within the month. Though I had always felt inspired by my mother's service in Africa, I was now seeing the ripple effect that such obedience can generate.

We need to watch out, then, in getting too comfortable in our material ease and "security." When we are content, we are less alert, less likely to take risks, however precious the gains, less willing to stretch and strive for excellence. Much of our vitality can die in the lap of comfort or contentment, which we confuse with achievement. Accepting our circumstances, whatever they are, with a sense of peace is a wise way to look at life. At the same time, we can remain alert. We can be willing to take measured risks, to stretch ourselves, and to reach for excellence. The goal is acceptance, while staying alert and aware of attitudes through which we can grow. And the caution is about contentment, which lulls us into wasting our lives.

In Revelation 3:17, we are told, "Because you say, 'I am rich, and have become wealthy, and have need for nothing,' and you do not know that you are wretched and miserable and poor and blind and naked." Ask yourself, in turn, "If I am rich and lack for nothing, why should I feel any need for God?" Herein lies the great danger of wealth: the arrogance and self-centeredness that wealth can facilitate.

Jason was smart and lucky in an investment he made in his early twenties. By the time he was thirty, he had $50 million. He waited to marry until he found a woman who could give him the social prestige he lacked, and even more importantly, she was a woman who had her own inherited wealth. Above all, he did not want any woman taking the wealth he had. She, on the other hand, had very expensive tastes and lavish spending habits. She was actually quite insecure and wanted much more material wealth than she already had. When

Jason and Meg married, at first it seemed like they both had gotten what they wanted. The couple had two children, and this was when the spiritual challenges began to reveal themselves.

Jason found that he had married a woman who, despite her efforts to address her insecurities with more material acquisitions, also had some spiritual stirrings, which were intensified by the arrival of children. She believed that somehow she needed to provide religious guidance for her children. She wanted to take them to church. This annoyed Jason greatly. He thought church was for the weak and wanted nothing to do with it. To her surprise, the more he resisted, the more important she felt the spiritual guidance of her young children to be. Though she tried to back up and regard God as unimportant, she couldn't, and she came to feel that a wedge had been driven into their marriage. She even said, "If we ever get a divorce, it will be because he is completely closed to our family being spiritual at all."

Professional observations: Jason has allowed his wealth to insulate him from the very personal growth that could make his marriage truly rich. The quest for the next bigger and better toy has engulfed him. It is normal for couples to grow and struggle to grow together in new ways. But Jason's limitations may take him all the way to divorce court and the demise of his family.*

> The danger lies not in wealth itself but in the overbearing assumptions we make about our relevance and importance *because* of our wealth.

The danger lies not in wealth itself but in the overbearing assumptions we make about our relevance and importance *because* of our wealth. It is this arrogance and sense of self-importance that is loathsome in God's eyes and that will keep us from entering the kingdom of heaven as surely as the camel is kept from passing through the eye of a needle.

We need to remember that we came into the world with nothing and we will leave with nothing. So, if you have been given material riches by God, realize also that you have been handed an exquisite two-part challenge: (1) how to use your financial wealth to glorify God—please think broadly in addition to churches and other deserving institutions—while (2) keeping your material attachments in check so you retain your awareness of what is really important in life and thereby keep your attention focused on God.

We shouldn't expect much support in these worthwhile endeavors from our worldly friends and relatives, particularly those so-called "movers and shakers." In considering their influence on your efforts to focus on God, have you noticed their jaded irreverence? Have you noticed how trendy their priorities are?

In Proverbs 30:7–9, Agur is praying for circumstances that will help him develop character. He prays, "Two things I asked of Thee, Do not refuse me before I die: Keep deception and lies far from me; Give me neither poverty nor riches; feed me with the food that is my portion, Lest I be full and deny Thee and say, 'Who is the Lord?' Or lest I be in want and steal, and profane the name of my God."

In yet another human attempt to cope with the difficulty of keeping our awareness of the Lord foremost in our lives, Agur asks God to give him the portion that is his due, not so much that he would deny God, and not so little that he would be tempted to be completely distracted by sin. This is the delicate balance for which we must strive, for as inheritors of financial wealth, we have been given the opportunity to shine in ways that the materialistic world does not value. But herein lies the challenge. Mainly, it is one of achieving excellence with humility in accordance with the gifts accorded us.

Jesus taught about the importance of humility by lauding artless virtues. With a child by his side, he told worshipers, "Whoever then humbles himself as this child, he is the greatest in the kingdom of heaven" (Matthew 18:4). God wants us to understand that human qualities such as trust, openness, and humility will be rewarded in heaven: "For he who is least among you, this is the one who is great" (Luke 9:48). And in Mark 9:35, Jesus said, "If anyone wants to be first, he shall be last of all, and servant of all."

For inheritors, their wealth, which represents power in our culture, can deliver a challenge of self-discipline to hold this attitude of humility in the forefront of their awareness. It is important as well for us to understand the difference between humility and self-consciousness, embarrassment, or shame. Make no mistake about it: Humility is a strength; its impostors are weaknesses.

Still another aspect of humility is yielding to God's will. True, it is not always obvious what God's will is for each of us, but as we study the Word, the path God has planned for each of us becomes clearer.

Lisa was plainly adrift when I first met her. She was a sweet young woman in her early twenties without much sense of purpose or direction. She had grown up as the only child of a divorce, receiving little guidance and a complicated inheritance to manage. Hoping to get some bearings in her aimless experience, she came to one of my workshops.

Often a searching for some sense of purpose in life reveals a spiritual awakening, like the tip of an iceberg surfacing in an uncharted sea. And so it was for Lisa. She asked to talk privately about her search for meaning and direction, and we started to explore these awakenings of spirituality in her. She had come to a crossroads in her young life and wanted to make a commitment in her spiritual journey: a choice, perhaps, of a religious practice. As it turned out, Lisa wasn't ready for such a commitment but resolved herself, instead, to a plan of study that would lead her forward. She did this on her own, only needing some encouragement.

Professional observations: *Many people feel a need for privacy as they begin to awaken spiritually. Some people have a sense of having resisted this dimension of their lives and worry about the ripple effect of opening the door. Others feel the self-consciousness of being a beginner at anything. Still others are simply curious and are extremely motivated; privacy may be far less important. The quest for a sense of purpose isn't always a spiritual awakening, but many times it is.*

Yielding to God's will often causes us to share with God rejection by the self-centered world. And, often, this submission means sharing in God's suffering and humiliation. In following God's example, sometimes we feel as if we are *losing* rather than gaining something, but if we can let go of that feeling of loss we will gain more than we could have imagined. How many times do we miss God's blessings by clinging to what *we* think is good for us instead of trusting that God's blessings come in ways we often aren't looking for?

Years ago, I heard a moving story about a young man I'll call James, who was graduating from college. His father was a wealthy man who had given his son many opportunities to earn the things he wanted. Nonetheless, James thought he deserved a sports car as a graduation present—a luxurious gift, true, but he knew the cost would be inconsequential for a man of his father's means. So he picked out the car he wanted and told his father about the object of his desire and the dealership where he had found it.

James immediately began picturing himself driving his sports car, imagining how "cool" he would look. (Haven't we all done that, before the fact?) By the time graduation day arrived, James had worked himself into a state of excitement over his graduation gift. When the family returned home after the graduation ceremony and festivities, James's father asked him to join him in his study.

Upon entering the room, the father said, "Son, please sit down. I have an important gift for you. I hope you'll treasure it for every-thing it can be in your life." With this, he held out a wrapped gift, which his son opened eagerly. James's spirits plummeted when he saw that the box contained a beautifully bound Bible. Barely con-taining his disappointment, the young man thanked his father as best he could, and then he promptly left to start his adult life.

It was many, many years later, shortly after his father's death, that James came across the Bible again, covered with dust on a shelf in the attic where he had put it. Seeing the Bible brought back the keen disappointment and loss he had felt on that graduation day long ago. Picking it up, James brushed away the dust and opened it for the first time. As he absentmindedly turned the pages, his mind reflecting on the events of that distant day, something fell into his lap. He looked down and saw the ignition key to the sports car on which he had set his heart so long ago.

Professional observations: *It is so easy to let our own wills rule our lives. We think we know what's best for us, yet we cannot fathom how limited our perceptions are. James knew his father to be a loving man, and yet in regard to the important challenge of spiritual growth he did not allow his father to guide him in that critical period of young adulthood. When in doubt, open the Bible. You aren't likely* *to find the key to a sports car there, but you* will *find other kinds of keys, and they will be the ones you need.*

In another parable in the book of Matthew (20:1–16), Jesus tells the story of a wealthy landowner who hired laborers to work in his vineyard, beginning at various times of the day. Each worker agreed to the same wage as all the others: one denarius (a silver coin of ancient Rome which represented the normal pay for a day's work).

At the end of the day, however, as the landowner paid all the workers, the first ones hired became upset when they realized they were being paid the same amount for their long, hard day's work in the scorching heat as the last laborers hired, who had worked only the few remaining hours of the day.

The warning this story holds for us is that we should be careful about assuming what we deserve. The story is actually about God's grace, and God (represented by the landowner in this parable) offers us all an equal amount of it. Not only does God set no provision for earning grace, but God also tells us that this generosity is not our province—God chooses to offer the same to everyone.

We need to be careful, therefore, of assuming what we deserve or don't deserve from God. We need to be careful as well, the parable cautions, of thinking that someone else deserves less or more than we do, for whatever reason. God decides what we deserve, not us. That is the simple, powerful moral of this story.

~

At this juncture in your understanding of all this, you may ask, "Well, then, how do I *do* this difficult thing? How do I replace the security I derived from my material wealth with security in God?" This, needless to say, is a question which can only be answered personally. Some have tried to answer it by giving away all or most of their money. Saint Francis is one of the best known among those who have given away wealth and income. He earned a place of honor in the tradition of hermits and monks who just get rid of it. It is a clear-cut model of divestment. Such altruism, while simplifying the dilemma, is too uncomfortable a choice for many.

For most of us, the answer lies in increasing our awareness, understanding, and discipline in improving our attitudes and behaviors. In Acts 20:35, Paul reminds us that Jesus said, "It is more blessed to give than to receive." The model of Jesus, too, is divestment. In fact, giving is essential to spiritual health. There are two reasons to give: (1) in a world of hunger and scarcity we don't want to show up on Judgment Day with millions of dollars in our names, because it's a definite liability, and (2) it's so much fun to invest creatively for the good of others. There are opportunities in very poor areas of this country and other countries where you can invest a relatively small amount by American standards and be absolutely awed and humbled at how much good it can do.

Another model has been created by Millard Fuller, the founder of Habitat for Humanity. This is a program which helps others on many levels, everyone from the recipients of the house that is built, to the workers who have the privilege of donating their expertise and/or labor to help, to the donors who provide the funds, to the organizers who do a tremendously fulfilling job.

Other individuals come up with their own strategic investments, or they join one of the many organizations which exist for the purpose of dispersing wealth to legitimate, underfunded charitable causes, or they start foundations. There are many exciting and creative ways to divest yourself of the wealth you have chosen to devote to the good of others.

There is no hurry. One of the best ways to get started is by getting to know God better. And getting to know God better works best when we prioritize our relationship with God, placing it higher than anything else in our lives.

We must, therefore, regardless of how we handle the challenge of our material wealth, specifically, intentionally, and methodically build our spiritual practice. In short, we must allow our spirituality to take up more and more of our time, attention, and affection. In Matthew 19:26, Jesus encourages the disciples, who were astonished at Jesus' earlier words describing the difficulty of a rich person entering the kingdom of God, by telling them that what may appear impossible to them is not necessarily so. "With God all things are possible," Jesus assures them. For it is God who creates a way for everyone, rich or poor, to enter into heaven. And it is through our faith that we all enter.

Each of us has a god, and it is not necessarily the God of the Bible. Your god is simply who or what you value the most in your life, who or what you prioritize the highest, who or what you think about when making your difficult decisions, who or what you instinctively turn to for help when you're in trouble. This god, therefore, could very well be your family, your spouse, or your wealth, to name a few possibilities.

Each of us has a god, and it is not necessarily the God of the Bible.

If you haven't made a conscious decision about who or what your god is, it doesn't necessarily mean you don't have one—only that you're not aware of who or what it is. Actually, many people think their god is the God of the Bible, when it really isn't. If you were privy to an inside view of their private lives, you would find that in reality their god is money or family or work or some other object of pursuit or desire. Again, it is whatever they think about the most. When you find God in a positive, spiritual context, you find your surest path out of the dark side.

⌒

Some people resist the spiritual teaching they have received. The resistance may stem from the hypocrisy they perceive in some of their religious friends. Or it may come from abuse encountered in their lives that, for them, mocks the notion of the benevolent God they wish for. Or their resistance may come from previous mis-understandings or adverse experiences connected with "religion."

Yet when the tide finally turns, when these people finally become motivated to make a spiritual commitment and to develop a spiritual practice, often their newfound conviction equals the strength of their former resistance. For the development of spiritu-ality always involves the growth of a spiritual backbone, a process that often includes disillusionment and unhappiness. In other words, if we have nothing worth struggling for, i.e., joy, fulfillment, and serenity in our lives, why should we struggle at all? This, too, is part of the inheritor's unique challenge in life.

At my church, there is wonderful sign posted outside the fifth-grade classroom. It says, "What is popular is not always right. What is right is not always popular." Amen, I say to myself when-ever I read those words, for they always make me reflect on my conviction that what is right is more important. We search for values in common in relationships, and the more consciously and carefully we do that, the better are our chances of building healthy ones. And we must always guard against doing the popular thing simply to win the acceptance of those we esteem in our lives.

What we do to gain that acceptance must also be right. Another name for this is *character*.

By the same token, as we mature spiritually, we find that our beliefs influence how we interact with others and how we are perceived by the world around us. For me, kindness has always been the greatest measure of a person's worth. It is the most important of all the attitudes and behaviors that we can exemplify as individuals who bear the imprint of God. There are, of course, many ways to express kindness, and one of the most meaningful for inheritors is philanthropy.

Philanthropy often starts as a spark of inspiration, which brightens into a sense of expansiveness in which one sees opportunities to help make the world a better place for one person or for many, and often it becomes a specific act or even cycle of benevolence. Philanthropy, however, is more than the giving of one's time, talents, or treasures. Most importantly, it is your manifestation of God's Word through kindness and love. As inheritors explore philanthropy, some reach the point of asking, "What will I be remembered for, and how does this affect choices about my life in the present?"

Needless to say, the primary reward of genuine altruism, defined in the dictionary as "the principle or practice of *unselfish* concern for the welfare of others," is spiritual in nature. When givers remark that their rewards are tenfold, a hundredfold, or more, they are referring to their spiritual experience of giving. An interesting test for the philanthropist, then, is to consider whether you can make your gift anonymous. This is an exercise in knowing that your act is purely a reflection of your love of God and a completely private matter between you and God.

When you are able to enjoy exploring the possibilities you find for philanthropy, and when you make a decision with confidence to give money to help others, you are making a statement. The statement is that you know you are OK.

There are many wonderful resources to guide and inspire the novice philanthropist. You will find some of them listed in the resource section in the back of this book.

CHAPTER ELEVEN

Making the Best of a Good Situation

IN CONCLUSION, let me sum up the best advice I can give you for leading a long, rewarding, fulfilling, worthwhile life as an inheritor:

Go slowly as you put together your team of advisors. Take time interviewing at least three of each of the following: financial planners, accountants, investment advisors, and estate-planning attorneys. In each case, wait until you experience a true rapport with an individual, and can imagine *looking forward* to meetings, before you hire him or her.

Let awareness be your first step. Interviewing your team of advisors may be your awakening. Stretch. Ask every question you can think of, even the elementary or "dumb" ones. This is the process of waking up.

Seek the help of a therapist. You may think you don't need one, and possibly you don't; just keep in mind that you are facing many important changes in your life, some of which you never anticipated or even dreamed could be possible. A therapist can be your sounding board and guide on your journey, providing you focus, awareness, direction, and accountability.

Guidance is key for inheritors. Make sure the inheritors in the next generation have strong and clear guidance such as incentive trusts, religious upbringing, and/or extensive parental commitment and involvement. A new inheritor without guidance will quickly fall prey to the pull of the world and get into trouble, probably losing the wealth as well.

Check your values. Imagine you have only one week to live. What will you do with your precious week? This is a great way to find out what is important to you and how well you have your actions lined up with your values and priorities. When you do this exercise, write out your answer and keep the pages so you can look back over them at a later date.

Learn to manage stress well. Review your values. Clarify and check them on a regular basis (such as on an annual vacation or New Year's Day). And set your priorities according to your values. Then base your actions on your priorities. Include exercise and focused relaxation in every day.

Develop your spiritual life. If you don't have a spiritual practice already, develop one. This is not optional. To find true happiness and fulfillment and to create a balanced life, you need to have a spiritual practice. This is what will take you to a perspective greater than your own individual ego so you can remember what we're here for, what it's all about.

Work. Hard. Hang in there when the going gets tough. Competence is the goal. The successful inheritor will go through whatever it takes to acquire competence in his or her chosen field. We all need to have meaningful work. Work is its own reward.

Find ways to make your life your own. Don't let your life be about not losing the money. Educate yourself enough to be a good steward, don't take financial risks you don't understand, and do put your time and attention into work where you can make a difference.

Take care of your relationships. Learn to forgive. Forgiveness is the single most powerful tool any of us has. Remember, it is a process and you can get help with it. In taking care of your relationships with others you will be taking care of your relationship with God.

Look at your greatest resistance. Stop! Before you read on, bring that troubled thought to mind ...

Now, remember, where there is the most resistance, there is the most potential for acceptance, forward motion, and personal growth.

Make a commitment to be the best you can be. Since wealth typically exaggerates whatever character traits you have, positive or negative, you have a great responsibility to develop the ones you want to shine forth. You have the privilege (or the curse) of making big statements with your character.

Be grateful. At a regular time every day, acknowledge five things for which you are grateful. Look for opportunities throughout each day to practice gratitude.

Be of service to others. Develop both the attitude and the practice of service to others. It will guard you against the attitude of entitlement.

Attitude is the name of the game. You have the power to choose your attitude about everything in your life. You may not have the awareness or the skills yet to make choices about your attitudes, but you can get them if you work at it. Ask the wisest person you know to help you. Remember, wealth is absolutely relative. This underscores the importance of attitude.

Psalm 37:4. Read it often. Believe it. *Live* it.

Resources

Books

Brooks, Robert, and Sam Goldstein. *Raising Resilient Children: Fostering Strength, Hope and Optimism in Your Child.* Chicago: Contemporary Books, 2001.

Collier, Charles W. *Wealth in Families.* Cambridge, Mass.: Harvard University, 2002.

Domini, Amy, Dennis Pearne, and Sharon Rich. *The Challenges of Wealth: Mastering Personal and Financial Conflicts.* Dow Jones/Irwin, 1988. Order directly from the author at *dpearne@aol.com.*

Ellis, Charles D. *"Winning the Loser's Game": Timeless Strategies for Successful Investing.* New York: McGraw-Hill, 1998.

Hausner, Lee. *Children of Paradise: Successful Parenting for Prosperous Families.* Order directly from the author at *www.dhvadvisors.com.*

Hughes, James E., Jr. *Family Wealth: Keeping It in the Family.* Princeton, N.J.: Bloomberg Press, 2004.

Nicholson, William. *Shadowlands.* New York: Plume, 1991. *Shadowlands* is a play about giving up the shield of the comfortable and familiar, growing up, and learning to love.

Ruiz, Don Miguel. *The Four Agreements.* San Rafael, Calif.: Amber-Allen Publishing, 1997. *The Four Agreements* will help you reflect on your values.

Smedes, Lewis. *Forgive and Forget: Healing the Hurts We Don't Deserve.* New York: HarperCollins, 1996.

Stanny, Barbara. *Prince Charming Isn't Coming: How Women Get Smart about Money.* New York: Penguin, 1997.

The Inheritance Project / Trio Press

Ten publications—three books and seven booklets—are helpful resources for wealthy parents, inheritors, and their professional advisors. These publications are not in bookstores. Order from the Web site at *www.inheritance-project.com* or call 902-431-8890 for information.

Philanthropy

Changemakers

www.changemakers.org
1550 Bryant Street, Suite 850, San Francisco, California 94103
415-551-2363

Changemakers is a national foundation dedicated to transforming the values and practice of philanthropy in order to ensure a more equitable and accountable distribution of resources for creating positive social change. Through grantmaking, donor education, and other programs, Changemakers seeks to (1) build the capacity of organizations practicing and promoting community-based philanthropy, (2) expand the number of donors and dollars supporting social change, and (3) transform philanthropy by promoting the values and practices of community-based philanthropy in the larger philanthropic sector.

Habitat for Humanity

www.habitat.org

121 Habitat Street, Americus, Georgia 31709

229-924-6935

Habitat for Humanity is a Christian organization with the goal of eliminating poverty housing from the face of the earth. Volunteer opportunities are available through any one of several thousand affiliates in this country and around the world. You may contact your local affiliate.

Resourceful Women

www.rw.org

P. O. Box 29423, San Francisco, California 94129

415-561-6520

Resourceful Women offers education and peer support for women who give more than $25,000 annually.

World Vision

www.worldvision.org

P. O. Box 9716, Federal Way, Washington 98063-9716

1-800-426-5753

World Vision was founded in 1950 to help children orphaned in the Korean War and continues to help children realize their full potential by tackling root causes of poverty. It has grown to become a global leader in delivering Christian humanitarian aid, and last year it served more than 60 million people in nearly 100 countries including the United States of America.

Organizations for further resources

More Than Money

www.morethanmoney.org
P. O. Box 1094, Arlington, Massachusetts 02474
781-648-0776

More Than Money is a national nonprofit organization that helps people explore the emotional, spiritual, and practical impact of wealth in their lives through conferences, events, coaching, and a quarterly journal. More Than Money supports a "Wealth Counselor Network." Contact them to locate a wealth counselor in your area.

World Vision *(listed under "Philanthropy" above)*

World Vision also offers resources for donor education as well as financial and legal advice.

Contact the author

Thayer Willis

www.thayerwillis.com
New Concord Press
P. O. Box 3825
Portland, Oregon 97208-3825

About the Author

THAYER CHEATHAM WILLIS is an internationally recognized author and expert in the area of wealth counseling. Since 1990, she has specialized in helping people of all ages handle the psychological challenges of wealth. Born into the founding family of the multi-billion-dollar Georgia-Pacific Corporation, she has a unique insider's perspective on the privileges and tragedies that wealthy families deal with on a regular basis. Willis has an M.A. from the University of Oregon, an M.S.W. from Portland State University, and a License in Clinical Social Work. She is a very popular speaker, facilitator, and counselor, and she is famous for her caring, no-nonsense, practical approach to resolving conflict. Clients have highly rated her interactive approach based on field-tested ideas that clarify understanding, problem-solving, and action-planning. She helps people create pathways between generations, prioritize parenting tasks, and instill financial responsibility in young family members. Thousands have attended her presentations ranging from small groups to top corporations and organizations including many private family retreats, the NAPFA National Conference, The Capital Trust Company of Delaware, The Gathering, and the Morgan Stanley Senior Consultants' Conference. Her programs are customized for families, attorneys, and financial professionals. Her book, *Navigating the Dark Side of Wealth: A Life Guide for Inheritors* (New Concord Press), has received rave reviews. Her professional affiliations are with the Family Firm Institute, the Family Wealth Alliance, and the National Speakers Association.

Index